A Lutheran's Case for Roman Catholicism

A Lutheran's Case for Roman Catholicism

Finding a Lost Path Home

Robert C. Koons

CASCADE *Books* • Eugene, Oregon

A LUTHERAN'S CASE FOR ROMAN CATHOLICISM
Finding a Lost Path Home

Copyright © 2020 Robert C. Koons. All rights reserved. Except for brief quotations in critical publications or reviews, no part of this book may be reproduced in any manner without prior written permission from the publisher. Write: Permissions, Wipf and Stock Publishers, 199 W. 8th Ave., Suite 3, Eugene, OR 97401.

Cascade Books
An Imprint of Wipf and Stock Publishers
199 W. 8th Ave., Suite 3
Eugene, OR 97401

www.wipfandstock.com

PAPERBACK ISBN: 978-1-7252-5749-8
HARDCOVER ISBN: 978-1-7252-5750-4
EBOOK ISBN: 978-1-7252-5751-1

Cataloguing-in-Publication data:

Names: Koons, Robert C., author.

Title: A Lutheran's case for Roman Catholicism : finding a lost path home / Robert C. Koons.

Description: Eugene, OR: Cascade Books, 2020 | Includes bibliographical references and index.

Identifiers: ISBN 978-1-7252-5749-8 (paperback) | ISBN 978-1-7252-5750-4 (hardcover) | ISBN 978-1-7252-5751-1 (ebook)

Subjects: LCSH: Catholic Church—Relations—Lutheran Church. | Catholic Church—Doctrines—History. | Lutheran Church—Relations—Catholic Church. | Lutheran Church—Doctrines—History.

Classification: BT764.2 .K60 2020 (print) | BT764.2 (ebook)

Manufactured in the U.S.A.   AUGUST 21, 2020

To my many Lutheran forebears, who faithfully passed on to me the sacrament of baptism and the fundamentals of the Christian faith.

Table of Contents

Preface ix
Introduction xi
1. The burden of proof 1
2. The question of justification 10
    2.1 What exactly is at issue 10
    2.2 The case for the Lutheran side 14
        2.2.1 Justification as forensic 14
        2.2.2 Grace as favor vs. grace as help 22
        2.2.3 Faith, not works 22
        2.2.4 Faith as "passive" and "merely receptive" 30
        2.2.5 The no-boasting argument 33
        2.2.6 The distinction between Law and Gospel 33
        2.2.7 *Solo Christo* 36
        2.2.8 Simultaneously saint and sinner 37
        2.2.9 Meriting an increase in grace is a self-contradiction 38
        2.2.10 Post-Vatican II Neo-Pelagianism 40
        2.2.11 The motivation for good works 40
    2.3 The case for the Roman Catholic side 41
        2.3.2 Salvation as a reward 41
        2.3.4 The fatal contradiction in the Lutheran position 44
    2.4 Eternal vs. temporal penalties, purgatory 46
    2.5 Self-righteousness and the assurance of salvation 50
    2.6 In summary: the crux of the matter 54
3. *Sola Scriptura* 59
    3.1 The case for the Lutheran position 61

Table of Contents

    3.2 The case for the Roman Catholic position 66
    3.3 The historic episcopacy 70
    3.4 Infallibility 73
4. Other Issues 75
    4.1 Purgatory and praying for the dead 75
    4.2 Praying to the saints 76
    4.3 Mary 77
    4.4 The Mass as a sacrifice 80
    4.5 The primacy of the pope 81
Conclusion 85
Epilogue 87
Appendix A: Commentary on the Council of Trent 89
    Session V 89
    Session VI 91
        Decree on Justification 91
        Canons 106
Appendix B: Commentary on Proof Texts concerning Justification by Faith 117
    I. Lutheran Proof Texts 117
        A. Pauline Epistles 117
        B. Other Texts 128
    II. Roman Catholic Proof Texts 132
        A. Justification includes Sanctification: Not Merely Forensic 132
        B. The Sanctified Fulfill the Law 135
        C. Rewards Based on Good Works 136
Appendix C: St. Augustine's *The Spirit and the Letter* on Justification as Inherent Righteousness 141
Bibliography 147
Scripture Index 149
General Index 153

Preface

I WROTE THE FOLLOWING essay in early 2006 while still a member of the Lutheran Church-Missouri Synod. On the Vigil of Pentecost in AD 2007 (May 25) I was formally received into the fellowship of the Roman Catholic Church at the parish of St. Louis the King of France in Austin, Texas.

The essay began as a set of private notes written as a purely intellectual exercise: an attempt to exorcise my doubts about Lutheranism by putting them to paper and exposing them to critique (both on my part and on that of others). As it turned out, the more I wrote, the more reasons I found for changing my outlook.

Bear in mind that I am no professional theologian, and I claim no special authority for my conclusions. I welcome feedback, but I would ask that my readers take a look first at John Henry Newman's book, *An Essay on the Development of Doctrine* (1845). Newman's book is essential background reading for my notes, because he provides the decisive rebuttal to the argument that the supremacy of the pope and other contemporary, distinctively Roman Catholic doctrines constitute objectionable "innovations." Newman convincingly argues that the recognition of genuine development in Christian doctrine is inescapable, as anyone who knows the history of the doctrines of the Trinity and the two natures of Christ must recognize.

One more thing about my notes: they were written with an audience of one (myself) in mind. In writing them, I gave no thought to being diplomatic or irenic. My only point was to try to sort out which of the two traditions was more likely to be the

Preface

fullest expression of the gospel. They are deliberately one-sided: there is much that I could have said about the virtues of the Lutheran tradition and the need for the reformation of the sixteenth-century Church not included here.

I have decided not to add or revise my comments now that I have joined the Church of Rome. I have left the essay as written by my earlier, Lutheran self. There is one lacuna in my argument for the historic episcopate that I would, if I were writing it now, attempt to fill. My argument takes essentially the following form:

(1) God wills that the Church be (visibly) one.

(2) Whoever wills the end wills some effective means.

(3) The only effective means for the visible unity of the Church is the historic episcopacy.

Therefore, God wills the historic episcopacy.

There is an obvious flaw with this sort of argument when applied to the will of God: an omnipotent God can use any means, or no means at all, to achieve his ends. Hence, (2) and (3) must be modified:

(2') If God wills an end for X, he must will some effective means that is appropriate to the nature of X.

(3') The only effective means for the visible unity of the Church that is appropriate to human nature is the historic episcopacy.

The rationale for (3') lies in the fact that human beings are essentially social or "political" animals, as Aristotle argued. God could have preserved the visible unity of the Church by supernaturally guiding each individual Christian to the right theological standards, but such supernatural intervention at the level of the individual member would destroy the social character of the Church, a result deeply antithetical to human nature. As St. Thomas so often taught us, grace perfects and does not annihilate nature (*gratia naturam, non tollit, sed perfecit*).

Introduction

I'VE ALWAYS THOUGHT THAT the doctrine of justification is the crux of the Lutheran/Catholic controversy. If the Roman Church has been in error on this point, to the extent of condemning the true understanding of the basis of our righteousness before God, then the Reformation was fully justified. Conversely, if Rome has not been in error, if her position can be charitably interpreted as a faithful exposition of the gospel and her condemnations (at Trent) as the rejection of genuine errors, then the Reformation, which destroyed the visible unity of the Church and broke ancient bonds of fellowship, could not be justified. All other issues are secondary: *sola scriptura*, the role of the papacy, purgatory, the veneration and invocation of the saints, and so on.

This rethinking of the issue of justification has been a long process, begun nearly thirty years ago, when I was an undergraduate student. This reflection was intensified in recent years by the Joint Declaration on the Doctrine of Justification, issued by Lutheran and Roman Catholic theologians in 1999, in which it was argued that the two Churches are in agreement on the essential points of this doctrine. In my view, the Joint Declaration was flawed, relying in places on equivocation and euphemism in place of clarity, but it did help to highlight the fact that the difference on this issue is much subtler than had been generally recognized by Lutherans.

I used to be confident that the teachings of Paul in Romans, Galatians, and Ephesians made it quite clear that the Roman position on justification was fundamentally wrong. I've come to have

INTRODUCTION

serious doubts about this, however, based in part on a recent scholarship about Paul's writings,[1] and partly on a better understanding of exactly what the Roman Church teaches. In addition, I've come to the conclusion that the Lutheran position on justification is an unstable one, incorporating at least one fatal self-contradiction.

Roman Catholics generally now agree that the Reformation was badly needed: that there were serious errors and abuses in the Church that needed to be corrected, and that the basic truths of the gospel had been obscured and needed to be reasserted. Some over-correction then occurred, as the opposition between the two was hardened by the political exigencies. In addition, the Roman Catholic Church corrected some of the most serious errors and abuses at the Council of Trent, and it has made great progress in recent years in restoring clarity and proportion to its teaching of the doctrines of grace and justification.

One of the most fundamental questions is this: should the teaching of the Roman Catholic Church be interpreted charitably or uncharitably? This is not merely a rhetorical question. There is a serious case to be made for subjecting the teachings of any Church to as uncharitable a construction as possible. It is the responsibility of the Church to proclaim the gospel with unmistakable clarity. If a Church's teaching can reasonably be interpreted in a way that brings them into conflict with the gospel, then that is a grave fault. The strongest case for the Reformation can be made along these lines: that the Roman Church at the time of Luther failed to maintain a proper sense of proportion (between, say, hell and purgatory, or temporal and eternal penalties) and failed to express clearly the intimate connection between Christ's righteousness and our justification. In particular, the teaching of the Church at that time, and even in the Council of Trent, could be understood as implying that all Christ accomplished for us was to supply us with the tools (spiritual helps and blessings) that we would need to obtain for ourselves an autonomous state of inherent righteousness that could, all by itself and apart from any relation to Christ and his righteousness, win for us God's favor and acceptance. Moreover,

---

1. Wright, *Paul*; Zetterholm, *Approaches to Paul*.

Introduction

it was easy to confuse our "meriting" God's grace with our earning God's acceptance, putting God himself under an obligation to reward us. Finally, an overemphasis on satisfaction, temporal penalties, and purgatory tended to obscure the good news of Christ's victory for us over sin, death, hell, and God's wrath.

However, to the extent that the justification for separation and protest is made along these lines, Lutherans must be willing with each new generation to reconsider the rationale for continued separation in light of the current state of the proclamation of the gospel by the Roman Catholic Church. In addition, we must bear in mind that the Roman Catholic theologian has available all of the infallible data of the Scriptures that are available to the Lutheran theologian. Roman theology adds to this data the infallible pronouncements of popes and councils, but it does not subtract from it. This means that the Roman Catholic should both interpret the Scriptures in light of the Church's teaching, and the Church's teaching in light of the Scriptures. For example, the teaching of Trent that the Mass is a sacrifice must be interpreted in light of the teaching in the Epistle to the Hebrews that Christ offered himself once and for all on the cross, leading to the insight that Trent must be talking about the sacramental "making present" of that one sacrifice (as the new *Catechism of the Catholic Church* explains). Similarly, the Council's teaching about justification through inherent righteousness has to be interpreted in light of the scriptural truth that our right standing before God depends on our being in Christ, the righteous one.

1

The Burden of Proof

WHEN I WAS A college student, a friend of mine invited me to join a group that was reading together some of the works of the Church Fathers—they were reading Cyprian when I joined them. This was a deeply disturbing experience for me, one from which I have never fully recovered, for I found that, contrary to my expectations, the early Fathers sounded much more Roman than proto-Lutheran. Further reading of the patristics when at Oxford and more recently has only confirmed this impression. It is clear beyond all reasonable doubt to me that Luther's, and by extension all of Protestantism's, teaching on justification, insofar as it differs from Roman Catholic theology, was truly novel. It was not simply the recovery of the Augustinian or pre-scholastic doctrine of the Church; it was an unprecedented innovation. If correct, Luther was the first major theologian to recover the true meaning of Paul's epistles.

Many Lutherans have disputed this charge of innovation. This raises an issue of fundamental importance: can the Lutheran doctrine of justification be found in the Fathers? Here we must resist the temptation to engage in what scientists call "cherry-picking" the data—citing proof texts in which Church Fathers insist that we are saved by faith and by the merits of Christ. These points aren't the ones in dispute. The crucial issue is this: is the righteousness by which the justified are justified an alien righteousness, the righteousness of Christ entirely outside of us (*extra nos*) and apart from regeneration and the new kind of life that results? This I can't find this anywhere before Luther. If we look at the corpus of Fathers who are typically cited by Lutherans—Clement of Rome, Ambrose, Basil, John Chrysostom, Augustine—we find that they all give to regeneration and to the fruits of the Spirit a role to play in our justification. In short, we find the Fathers affirming what Lutherans affirm, but not denying what Lutherans deny, and it is the denials rather than the affirmations that are in dispute in the conflict between Rome and the Lutherans.

Some examples:

> Those who were perfected in love by the grace of God have a place among the pious who shall be made manifest at the visitation of the kingdom of Christ ... [I]f we perform the commandments of God in the concord of love, that through love our sins may be forgiven. (Clement, *First letter to Corinth*, chapter 50)[1]

> Repentance without alsmsgiving is a corpse and is without wings. (John Chrysostom, *On Repentance and Almsgiving*, Homily 7)[2]

> "For in Jesus Christ neither circumcision availeth any thing, nor uncircumcision; but faith working through love." What is the meaning of "working through love"? Here he gives them a hard blow, by showing that this error had crept in because the love of Christ had not been rooted within them. For to believe is not all that is required, but also to abide in love. (John Chrysostom, *Commentary on Galatians*, Homily 5)[3]

---

1. Roberts and Donaldson, eds., *Ante-Nicene Christian Library: Translations of the Writings of the Fathers down to AD 325*, 43.
2. Chrysostom, *On Repentance and Almsgiving*, 103.
3. ww.newadvent.org/fathers/23105.htm.

> The faith that saves is faith working in charity... Faith without works is not sufficient for salvation... Mortal sins are forgiven through repentance, prayer and almsgiving... Even eternal life itself, which is surely a reward of good works, is called by the apostle "a gift of God." But a gift is not a gift at all if it is not made gratuitously. Consequently, we are to understand that even man's good deserts are themselves gifts of God. When, therefore, eternal life is bestowed because of them, what else is this but a return of grace for grace? (Augustine, *Enchiridion*, chapters 67, 69, 107).[4]

This point is admitted by both Martin Chemnitz (a second-generation Lutheran reformer and theologian, 1522–1586) and by Robert Preus, in his more recent book, *Justification and Rome*.[5]

An egregious example of this cherry-picking is found in German Lutheran Reformer Philipp Melanchthon's (1497–1560) quotations from St. Augustine's *On the Spirit and the Letter*.[6] Melanchthon picks out a few, brief excerpts from this text, arguing that they establish that the Lutheran doctrine of justification by faith alone (apart from love) is no innovation but is wholly continuous with Augustinian theology. To read the entirety of *On the Spirit and the Letter* after reading Melanchthon is shocking: in that work, Augustine explicitly rejects the very doctrine that Melanchthon claims to find there. The gap between the plain sense of Augustine's text and Melanchthon's construction of it is so great that I found my confidence in Melanchthon's good faith as a scholar and

---

4. Augustine, *Enchiridion on Faith, Hope, and Charity*, 79–80, 83, 125.

5. Chemnitz argues that one can find passages in the devotional and meditative writings of some of the Fathers that supports justification by faith, but he admits that, in every case, when one turns to the Fathers' more polemical and theological works, one finds many "unfortunate statements" that contradict the Lutheran position. Chemnitz, *Justification*, 53. According to Robert Preus, Luther's emphasis on justification was "new since apostolic times" (*Justification and Rome*, 121n8). In the same book, Preus also admits that it was "unknown to scholastic theology preceding the Reformation" (65), which scholastic theology was based on the writings of Augustine (45).

6. Melanchthon, *Apology of the Augsburg Confession*, Article IV, Book of Concord, 153.

teacher badly shaken. In appendix C, I provide a few quotations from *On the Spirit and the Letter* that make clear that in Augustine's we are saved by an infused grace that gives us an inherent righteousness consisting in the love of God.

Thomas Oden, a contemporary Methodist theologian, compiled *The Justification Reader* (2002) in order to persuade Protestants that they should not disregard the testimony of the ancient Church Fathers. Although this was not Oden's primary intention, Oden's book could be taken as a defense of the catholicity of the doctrine of justification by faith alone, demonstrating that the doctors of the Church have continuously affirmed it. However, Oden fails to distinguish between the thesis that faith is *necessary* for justification and the thesis that faith is *sufficient*. Oden's textual evidence clearly supports the first thesis but utterly fails to support the second. The Lutheran and Reformed doctrine that we are justified by faith alone corresponds exactly to the sufficiency of faith. The necessity of faith (in opposition to the Pelagian heresy) was readily conceded by the Council of Trent.

For example, Oden quotes Origen:

> A man is justified by faith. The works of the law can make no contribution to this. Where there is no faith which might justify the believer, even if there are works of law, these are not based on the foundation of faith. Even if they are good in themselves, they cannot justify the one who does them, because faith is lacking, and faith is the mark of those who are justified by God.[7]

Although Origen does affirm that it is possible to be justified by faith without works (he mentions the thief on the cross), he goes on to warn that our works after conversion do have eternal consequences:

> But perhaps someone who hears these things should become lax and negligent in doing good, if in fact faith alone suffices for him to be justified. To this person we shall say that if anyone acts unjustly after justification, it is scarcely to be doubted that he has rejected the grace of

---

7. Oden, *Justification Reader*, 45.

justification. For a person does not receive the forgiveness of sins in order that he should once again imagine that he has been given a license to sin; for the remission is not given for future crimes, but for past ones.[8]

Oden's book establishes that the Fathers understood "freely" and "by grace" to mean that we cannot earn salvation—that we can give nothing "in return" for God's gift.

> We are saved by grace rather than works, for we can give God nothing in return for what is bestowed on us. (Jerome, *Epistle to the Ephesians* 1.2.1)[9]

> They are justified freely because they have not done anything nor given anything in return, but by faith alone they have been made holy by the gift of God. (Ambrosiaster, *Commentary on Paul's Epistles*)[10]

The Fathers teach that nothing of human merit precedes the gift of grace.

> Nothing of human merit precedes the grace of God, but grace itself merits increase ... (Augustine, Letter 186, to Paulinus)[11]

This also seems to be John Chrysostom's meaning in the one passage cited by Oden that comes close to affirming the Protestant doctrine:

> Does faith save without itself doing anything at all? Faith's workings are themselves the gift of God, lest anyone should boast. What then is Paul saying? Not that God has forbidden works but forbidden us to be justified by works. No one, Paul says, is justified by works, precisely in order that the grace and benevolence of God

---

8. Origen, *Commentary on the Epistle to the Romans*, book three, chapter 9.
9. Oden, *Justification Reader*, 48.
10. Oden, *Justification Reader*, 108. Ambrosiaster was a fourth-century Christian theologian writing under the name of "Ambrose of Milan."
11. Augustine, "Letter 186 to Paulinus," 10 (section 1446).

may become apparent. (Chrysostom, Homily 4 on Ephesians, 4:2.9)[12]

Chrysostom goes on, in the same homily, to say:

> Is God a God of loving-kindness? Yes, but He is also a righteous Judge. Is He one who maketh allowance for sins? True, yet rendereth He to every man according to his works. Doth He pass by iniquity and blot out transgressions? True, yet maketh He inquisition also. How then is it, that these things are not contradictions? Contradictions they are not, if we distinguish them by their times. He doeth away iniquity here, both by the laver of Baptism, and by penitence. There He maketh inquisition of what we have done by fire and torment.

Chrysostom clearly teaches that the sacraments of forgiveness, baptism and penance, blot out iniquities and enable us to merit eternal life by means of our subsequent works, the fruit of the Spirit. However, he does not establish that any of the Fathers thought of justification in terms of an external or "alien" righteousness, or that they denied that works are needed to persevere and to grow in grace.

There are two reasons why the Lutheran position must bear the burden of proof: the Lutheran doctrine was novel, and it precipitated a fragmentation[13] of the Church's unity. Both reasons are necessary: if the Lutherans had simply been rejecting a recent innovation, the division of the Church might be justified, as Athanasius's opposition to the temporary dominance of the Arians was. Alternatively, if the Lutheran position had become the object of a new worldwide consensus among Christians, reflected in the conclusions of an ecumenical council, this would have confirmed the

---

12. http://www.newadvent.org/fathers/230104.htm.

13. Is it unfair to blame the fragmentation on the Lutherans? It's certainly true that there is plenty of blame to place on both sides, and the ineptness of Leo X in dealing with the challenge of Luther contributed to the crisis. However, in the final analysis, it was the refusal of Lutherans to participate in the deliberations of the Council of Trent, or to accede to its demands, that constituted the schism.

The Burden of Proof

innovation as a legitimate *development of doctrine*, in John Henry Newman's sense. However, the only justification for a Church-dividing innovation would be the unmistakable and unambiguous affirmation of the doctrine by the Scriptures.

This burden of proof is compounded by the fact that the innovation led to the Lutherans' separating themselves from the majority of Christians in their day, and ours.[14] I grant that theological truth is not to be decided by majority vote. Athanasius was right to stand *contra mundum* (against the whole world). The conflict with the Arian heresy, which for a time dominated most of the established Church, is the best parallel for Lutherans to cite. Even in this case, though, two facts are striking. First, ecumenical councils of the Church were consistently Trinitarian; and, second, this fidelity to the Trinity is also true of the bishop of Rome. It's hard to believe that it has been a mere coincidence that both ecumenical councils and popes were consistently orthodox in rejecting each of the great heresies: Gnosticism, Arianism, Nestorianism, etc.

Lutherans have intentionally set aside at least one of the three pillars of orthodoxy (the consensus of the apostolic bishops), effectively disregarded the second (the rule of faith, reflected in the unanimous testimony of the Fathers), in favor of the third alone, the Scriptures. This can be defended only if the testimony of the Scriptures on the disputed points is unambiguous and unmistakable.

In addition, there is a real tension in the Lutheran position, which holds, on the one hand, that the doctrine of justification is the "article on which the Church stands or falls," and which also asserts, in defending infant baptism, that the Church has existed continuously from the time of the apostles. Given that we cannot find the Lutheran doctrine of justification among the pre-Reformation Church Fathers, we must conclude either that this doctrine is not essential to the gospel, or that the Church literally ceased to

---

14. I'm not ignoring the fact that it was Rome that first excommunicated the Lutherans. However, the fact remains that confessional Lutherans identify the true visible Church with those congregations they consider orthodox, effectively excluding the vast majority of Christians and all of the apostolic sees.

exist until revived at the time of the Reformation. The latter thesis is both in conflict with the Lutheran Confessions (especially Luther's defense of infant baptism in the Large Catechism) and in conflict with Jesus' promise to be with the Church until the very end (Matthew 28:20).

This tension could be put in another way. The Lutheran Church accepts the New Testament canon in accordance with the consensus of the Church as it developed over the first four centuries. Although Luther had some doubt about the Epistle of James, this doubt was explicitly rejected by the normative confessions of the Lutheran Church. Both Lutherans and Roman Catholics agree that it is not the authority of the Church that makes an inspired text a canonical one, but both agree that the testimony of the Church is a reliable guide to which books were in fact inspired. However, Lutherans must also hold that the early Church during this period was hopelessly confused about the central doctrine contained in the canonical books, the doctrine of justification by faith alone. Thus, Lutherans are in the awkward position of holding that the early Church was wholly reliable in recognizing which books were inspired and yet wholly unreliable in understanding what those books were saying. This seems inconsistent: how could the Church reliably recognize a book as God's Word without accurately understanding its meaning?

One might claim that the Reformation did not destroy the visible unity of the Church by arguing that the Scriptures teach that the true Church is always constituted by a divinely preserved "remnant." Thus, the Reformation simply freed the true Church from its captivity to a much larger but inauthentic "Church." However, all of the relevant scriptural references (including Romans 9) refer to the *remnant* as a part of the people established by the old covenant. The new covenant differs radically in a way that is pertinent: the law is now written in our hearts (Jeremiah), and the Holy Spirit is poured out upon all believers at Pentecost. Jesus' prayers for the Church and his instruction about the Comforter in the Gospel of John reinforce the importance of this new factor. The Holy Spirit will teach "you" (plural) all things and (John 14:26) lead "you" (plural) into all the truth (John 16:13). If the Church is collectively taught by the Holy Spirit and guided by the Holy Spirit into all the truth, we should not expect orthodoxy to be confined to a tiny remnant.

The Gospel of John gives us good reason to expect the Church to be both thoroughly orthodox and visibly united. The members of the Church are commanded to "love one another" (John 15:12), which presupposes a kind of visible unity (in particular, in the form of Eucharistic unity, i.e., fellowship in what the early Church called the *agape* meal). Jesus prays that the Father would sanctify "them" (plural) in the truth of his Word (John 17:19), and he prays that all who believe in him should be made "perfectly one"—visibly one, so that the world might believe in Christ (John 17:21–23).[15] It is only through the apostolic succession, centered in the successor of Peter in Rome, that the Church has been able to maintain both doctrinal discipline and global eucharistic unity. History demonstrates that Churches following the Protestant principle must sacrifice either one or the other: either choosing doctrinal purity over unity (conservatives) or choosing unity over purity (liberals and latitudinarians). Only through a visible authority (popes and councils) able to bring controversies to a decisive conclusion can the Church realize both of Christ's stated intentions for it.

---

15. Unless indicated otherwise (e.g., in Appendix B), I use the Revised Standard Version for my quotations of the Bible in English.

2

The Question of Justification

What exactly is at issue

THE GREATEST DIFFICULTY IN understanding the controversy is sorting out the different meanings that the two sides attach to the words *justification*, *grace*, and *faith*. All three words are understood in two fundamentally different ways, indicated here by R (Roman Catholic) and L (Lutheran).

- Justification (R) = the whole process by which sinners are reconciled, redeemed, and made fit for eternal life. Includes sanctification and glorification.
- Justification (L) = the process by which a sinner is reconciled to God, including the forgiveness of sins and the crediting to him of Christ's own righteousness. Excludes sanctification and glorification, which are, however, inseparable effects of it.
- Grace (R) = God's supernatural assistance, poured into the believer's heart, enabling him to possess the supernatural virtues of faith, hope, and love.
- Grace (L) = God's favor and forgiveness, undeserved by the sinner.

- Faith (R) = the supernatural ability to believe what God has revealed through the Scriptures and the Church. Does not include hope and love (although it finds its natural completion in them).
- Faith (L) = the supernatural ability to trust in God for one's salvation. Includes hope and an attitude of trust and reliance in God.

This variation in meaning greatly complicates things, making it seem that the two sides agree when they do not, and that they do not agree when they do. Thus, both sides will affirm that we are justified by grace alone, but they mean quite different things by this. Similarly, Lutherans affirm that we are justified through faith alone, while Catholics deny this, but this superficial disagreement fails entirely to capture the substance of the issue, since the two sides are not affirming and denying the same thing by the phrase "justification through faith alone."

In order to get clearer on the issues, I'll use the following terminology:

- Grace (R) = infused virtues (of faith, hope, and love)
- Grace (L) = undeserved favor
- Justification (R) = final salvation
- Justification (L) = reconciliation and acceptance
- Faith (R) = full doctrinal assent
- Faith (L) = personal trust

Thus, Rome teaches that final salvation is by infused virtue alone, but not through full doctrinal assent alone. Lutherans teach that reconciliation and acceptance by God are by undeserved favor through personal trust alone. Is there a disagreement here? As I understand it, Rome does not deny what Lutherans teach. Nor do Lutherans teach that our final salvation is by means of doctrinal assent alone. So far, no disagreement.

In addition, Rome teaches that salvation is the result (the normally expected result) of faith (in the narrow sense, doctrinal assent). In the Council of Trent, faith is described as the root and foundation of justification. Consequently, Rome has no difficulty with passages that describe salvation or justification as the result of faith: John 3:16, Ephesians 2:8, Romans 10:10. Nor is there any real disagreement on the question of whether all believers (understood by both Catholics and Lutherans to mean all who persevere in faith until death) will be saved. Rome teaches that sanctification is the natural result of persistence in faith (assuming a regular attendance to the sacraments, the means of grace), and Lutherans agree that saving faith is always accompanied by good works. Thus, "he who believes and is baptized will be saved" (Mark 16:16), "he who endures to the end will be saved" (Matthew 24:13), and "God will render to every man according to his works" (Romans 2:6). The disagreement lies, as we shall see, not in a dispute about which class of people will be saved, but about what the basis or ultimate reason for their justification consists in.

Lutherans will reject the very idea of Grace (R), infused virtue, as being instrumental in causing our final salvation (glorification). Lutherans will instead insist that infused virtue belongs to the process of sanctification, which is an effect of justification, but which has, in the end, nothing to do with our final destination. We are not glorified because we have been sanctified, but solely because we have been justified (L).

This disagreement could also be couched in terms of merit. Rome teaches that we must merit eternal life, but that we can do so only by means of the infused virtue of grace, not by means of our own unaided efforts. Lutherans teach that we merit eternal life only by having Christ's righteousness applied to us through justification. Our own inherent qualities and the actions that flow from them are completely irrelevant, even when those qualities in us are the direct result of divine help. However, this dispute also turns on a terminological confusion.

- Merit (L) = what is earned by the inherent moral quality of an action or person
- Merit (R) = what is rewarded by God, according to his gracious promises.

THE QUESTION OF JUSTIFICATION

Although a debt that is earned by labor or inherent quality is a kind of merit, Roman theology has always refused to identify the two. Roman theology recognizes two kinds of merit (condign and contiguous—more about this below), but neither kind involves a human being *earning* any compensation from God. This is true for two reasons: since God is infinite and we are finite, nothing we can do could possibly place God in our debt. Second, as a result of the fall, human beings are by nature incapable of doing anything worthy of God's acceptance, apart from regeneration and the gift of the Spirit, available only through faith in Christ.

Thus, when Roman theologians speak of our supernatural virtues or our supernaturally inspired works as "meriting" eternal life and other blessings, they do not mean to imply that eternal life is earned thereby. In fact, scholastic theology insisted that a thing's merit has nothing to do with its inherent moral or ethical quality. Rather, a human act or attribute "merits" reward only when God, out of his gracious mercy, has promised freely to do so.[1] As Alister McGrath notes, the later scholastic theologians understood merit in an ontological or causal sense (as that which acts as a means of God's grace), rather than in an ethical, forensic, or judicial sense.[2] Thus, if we translate Lutheran theology into Catholic language, we could legitimately say that our faith in Christ "merits" justification, and that the means of grace (the Word and sacraments) "merit" the remission of sins. Baptism merits regeneration, the remission of sins and the gift of the Spirit, not because there is any inherent quality in the event of being baptized, but solely because of God's promise.

Here's another attempt at isolating the issue: Lutherans insist that Christ's righteousness is "imputed" to us, and that it is this righteousness, and nothing inherent in us, that justifies us before God. To this, the obvious question is: if an omnipotent God "imputes"

---

1. This is a point on which the otherwise very reliable Norman Geisler and Ralph MacKenzie (*Roman Catholics and Evangelicals*) fall into error. They consistently interpret "merit" as meaning "partially earns," without providing any evidence for the correctness of this interpretation.

2. McGrath, *Justitia Dei*, 143.

Christ's righteousness to us, must this not make us really (i.e., inherently) righteous? When God said, "Let there be light," there was light. Similarly, if God says, "Let this Christian be righteous," must not this declaration make the Christian really righteous? To this, orthodox Lutherans answer, in one voice, Yes! So, there is a real righteousness in us that is effected by God's imputation to believers of Christ's own righteousness, and this inherent righteousness is something distinct from Christ's righteousness (since it is in us, and not in Christ). However, Lutherans insist that we are not *justified* by this inherent righteousness, but only (objectively speaking) by Christ's righteousness and (subjectively speaking) by our faith in Christ. In contrast, Catholics insist that the subjective basis of our justification is the inherent righteousness produced in us by God's imputation.

This is the heart of the issue. Who is right? Let's look first at the case for the Lutheran side.

The case for the Lutheran side

Justification as forensic

Lutherans appeal to the fact that the word *justify* in the Greek is primarily forensic in character. That is, it means to be declared or considered righteous, not to be made intrinsically righteous. Here there is little contemporary disagreement—the Lutherans are right here, and many Catholic theologians (beginning with Augustine himself) were confused by the translation of "justify" as "*justificare*" (to make righteous) by the Latin Vulgate.

However, Rome does not deny that we are, at our conversion, forensically declared righteous (and thereby adopted as God's children and incorporated into Christ) through our faith alone. First justification results in a new status, a new standing before God, as well as the infusion into our hearts of the Holy Spirit and his gifts of grace. This is in fact what many Catholics refer to as "first justification." First justification results in a new status, a new standing before God, as well as the infusion into our hearts of the

Holy Spirit and his gifts of grace. What the Romans deny is that the whole process of salvation ends with this forensic declaration and new status.

In fact, Lutherans don't really deny this, since Lutherans agree that all the saints in heaven will be intrinsically sinless. More importantly, Lutherans agree that the imputed righteousness given to faith in this life is not a mere fiction or supposition. When God declares someone righteous, the object of his declaration becomes, immediately, truly righteous as a result. In his *Disputation on Justification* (1536), Luther writes, "This imputation is not a thing of no consequence"; it is not a "game or delusion."[3] As the seventeenth-century Lutheran theologian Johannes Andreas Quenstedt put it, the imputation is "most real" (*realissima*), because it is an exercise of God's infallible word.[4] Lutherans deny, however, that this real righteousness involves a "grafting or indwelling,"[5] i.e., that the righteousness dwells in us "formally and intrinsically" (Quenstedt).[6] This aspect of Lutheran teaching is one that is difficult to make sense of, accounting for the fact that Lutherans are often misrepresented as teaching that imputed righteousness is merely a fiction. If God's declaration of our righteousness is necessarily effective, with the result that we are really righteous, how can it be that the righteousness does not in any sense dwell "within" us? If I really have an attribute (of righteousness), it is standard practice to say that that attribute is "in" me. What do Lutherans mean by denying this?

I think there are two closely related possibilities. First, let us look closely at what Luther writes in his 1535 *Commentary on Galatians*:

> Christ and my conscience become one body. Turning to myself and looking into myself, into what I am and ought to be and do, I lose sight of Christ, who alone is my

---

3. Luther, "Disputation on Justification," 167.

4. Quenstedt, *Theologia*, pars 1, cap. 8, sec. 5, q. 5. See Preus, *Justification and Rome*, 71–76, for more examples.

5. Balduin, *Commentarius in omnis Epistulas Beati Apostoli Pauli*, 78.

6. Quenstedt, *Theologia*, pars 1, cap. 8, sec. 5, q. 1.

righteousness and my life ... works, which only compel us to look to ourselves again, and turn our eyes from that brazen serpent, Christ crucified.[7]

Similarly, in a sermon in 1532, Luther writes:

> I feel in myself nothing but sin; and yet I am righteous and holy, not in myself, but in Christ Jesus who of God is made for me wisdom and righteousness and sanctification and redemption.[8]

In describing the righteousness we have in Christ as "alien" and "outside of us" (*extra nos*), Luther is pointing to the fact that this righteousness is not introspectible or internally "feelable." We do not find it by looking within, by examining our own consciousness or our works, but only by looking to Christ. Thus, it is "in" us in one sense, ontologically and metaphysically speaking, but it is "outside of" us in another sense, epistemologically and phenomenologically (that is, in terms of our knowledge and conscious experience). That the righteousness of Christ is in us ontologically is clear from Luther's reference to the "inseparable union and conjunction I have with Him through faith ... through faith you are so closely joined together with Christ that you and He are made one person."[9] If my esteemed reader will indulge me in the use of a little philosophical jargon, I would say that Luther and his followers made the understandable error of *ontologizing the phenomenology of faith*, that is, of inferring that what is true of our experience is necessarily true of the underlying reality.

A second related answer is that imputed righteousness is not wholly intrinsic to the believer: it involves essentially an extrinsic relationship to Christ. It is only because faith relates us to Christ that we are really righteous. Whatever state is internal to us constitutes righteousness only because of this connection to Christ. This answer is connected to the first, since it explains why the imputed

---

7. Luther, *Commentary on the Epistle to the Galatians*, 166.
8. Luther, "Sermon for the Feast of the Beheading of John the Baptist (1532)," 281–82. Author's translation.
9. Luther, "Lectures on the Epistle to the Galatians (1535)," 166.

righteousness can't simply be seen by introspection, but only by looking outward toward Christ.

Here is a distinction that might be helpful: between righteousness as *internal* reality and as an *intrinsic* fact. Since we become really righteous as a result of God's imputation to us of Christ's righteousness, this righteousness is (ontologically speaking) an internal reality. However, it is not a wholly intrinsic fact about us, as though the internal reality would constitute righteousness before God autonomously, apart from any connection to Christ. Given this distinction, the position of Lutherans and Catholics can be fully reconciled: both can agree that there is an internal righteousness that results from the imputation, but that we are not thereby intrinsically righteous (apart from our union to Christ). Here is how the recent Catechism of the Catholic Church puts it:

> *The charity of Christ is the source in us of all our merits* (emphasis in original) before God. Grace, by *uniting us to Christ* (emphasis added) in active love, ensures the supernatural quality of our acts and consequently their merit before God and man. (Paragraph 2011)[10]

The distinction between internal and intrinsic is not an empty one. Consider, for example, the fact of being married. One cannot be married without an appropriate internal state: one must know what is happening during the marriage ceremony and intend to be married in order for marriage to take place. For example, if someone participates in a marriage ceremony, thinking that he is merely rehearsing a play, a valid marriage does not result. At the same time, a marriage is not a wholly intrinsic fact: merely intending to be married or believing that one is married is not enough to constitute a true marriage. Marriage is partly constituted by external facts: a relation to one's spouse and to a legally valid public ceremony. In the same way, justification is constituted by an extrinsic relationship to Christ and his righteousness, but this state of justification must also correspond to a genuine internal reality. The only dispute between Roman Catholics and Lutherans concerns

---

10. Catechism of the Catholic Church, 487.

the exact nature of this internal reality: does it consist at all times of faith alone, or does it consist initially of faith but then progress into a state of faith working in love?

Both sides agree that our internal righteousness (whether faith alone, or love and the acts that flow from it) constitutes righteousness only because of our union with Christ. Of course, an obvious difference remains: is it our faith alone that unites us with Christ (Lutherans), or does the love that is poured into our hearts and the resulting works of love also play some role (Roman Catholics)?

Lutherans argue that Roman Catholics have confused justification itself from the fruits of justification. Lutherans identify our regeneration (including our new capacity to love God and neighbor) as a fruit of justification. Our regeneration does not unite us with Christ: it is rather the result of that justification.[11] However, there are strong grounds for thinking that it is really the Lutherans who are confused here. We should distinguish between that which God's imputation *effects* and that which it *causes*. For example, Oswald's killing of JFK *effected* JFK's death; it did not *cause* it. Oswald's killing of JFK (as opposed, say, to Oswald's shooting of him) includes JFK's death as an essential part: Oswald's killing of JFK was not complete until JFK had actually died. The effects of Oswald's killing of JFK (the things that it caused) include, not JFK's death, but the ramifications of that death, including the escalation of the Vietnam War. In the same way, imputation effects our regeneration; it does not cause it. Our regeneration is an essential part of God's imputation of Christ's righteousness to us; it is not merely the fruit of that imputation.

Both sides also agree that justification is inseparable from regeneration and the gift of the Holy Spirit. On the Catholic view, regeneration and justification are one and the same action,

---

11. Strictly speaking, this is only true of later Lutheran thought. In both the Augsburg Confession and in Melanchthon's *Apology*, the terms *justification* and *regeneration* are often used interchangeably. For example, in the *Apology of the Augsburg Confession*, articles II and III (Book of Concord, 37, 66, 68–69), Melanchthon explicitly identifies justification with the effecting of *regeneration*.

described from the point of view of the patient (regeneration) or the agent (justification). Lutherans insist that justification and regeneration are separate actions (Formula of Concord, Thorough Declaration III, Book of Concord, 251), the latter being merely the fruit of the former (although this distinction is not drawn in the Augsburg Confession or in Melanchthon's *Apology*). I don't find this separation taught anywhere in Scriptures or in the Fathers. It's a Lutheran innovation. (Ironically, the Lutheran insistence that regeneration follows justification by faith commits Lutherans to a kind of Pelagianism, since they ignore the fact that only the regenerate can trust God.)

However, isn't it by faith alone that the imputation occurs in the first place? Yes, the Roman Catholic Church agrees: the Council of Trent taught that faith is the "beginning," "root," and "foundation" of our justification.[12] Moreover, since nothing else is described in this way, Trent taught that faith alone is the root and foundation of justification: it is that *one* juncture with Christ through which all of the blessings of his life, death, and resurrection flow to the believer. Thus, there is one sense in which the Council of Trent, like the Book of Concord, teaches that we are justified by faith alone: faith plays a unique, foundational role in our justification. However, once the imputation has taken place, the imputed righteousness essentially includes the charity of God in our hearts, which then plays a causal role in maintaining our union with Christ. Consider, for example, Ephesians 2:8–9.

> For it is by grace that you have been saved (past perfect tense) through faith, and this is not your own doing, it is the gift of God—not because of works, lest any man should boast.

This passage from Ephesians refers to a past event that is already fully completed: our conversion, introduction to grace, what Romans refer to as our "first justification." This first justification is through faith alone. However, the state of justification does not *consist* solely of our faith in Christ: it includes essentially

---

12. Council of Trent, Sixth Session, chapter VIII.

the regeneration of the heart that is effected by God's imputation of righteousness to the believer. That this is so was conceded by Melanchthon's identification of *justification* and *regeneration* in the *Apology*, and by Luther's identification of justification with that *union* and *conjunction* of the believer with Christ that faith effects (as discussed above).[13]

The righteousness that is imputed to us is Christ's own righteousness. Christ's righteousness was not a wholly external matter: it surely included Christ's love for God and for people, his willing obedience to God, and his patient acceptance of suffering. If this very righteousness is imputed to us by God's declaration, then the righteousness we thereby acquire must be (at least in part) an internal affair. It must include our regeneration, the gift of the Spirit, and the indwelling of Christ himself (Galatians 2:20).

Moreover, if purely external righteousness were enough, why do we not remain both saints and sinners in heaven? Surely it is because there is something incompatible between sin and eternal blessedness. In order to enjoy the gift of heaven, we must at some point be purged our sin, made fit for God's presence. Through the imputation of Christ's righteousness, we are given all the resources (most crucially the gift of the Holy Spirit) needed to complete the process of sanctification. This is why, in Hebrews 10:14, we are told that Christ has already perfected us (past tense) who are being sanctified (present tense).

The core of the Lutheran position then, seems to be that this transformation (i.e., our final glorification) must occur instantaneously and willy-nilly at the death of the believer—that no active cooperation by us is involved. Lutherans in effect insist that sanctification has nothing to do with glorification—we are all equally and immediately glorified at death, regardless of how far our sanctification has progressed, and this final step requires no cooperation or suffering on our part. What is the scriptural basis for this claim? The only passage that comes close is Jesus' word to the thief in the cross, "Today you will be with me in paradise." (Luke 23:43)

---

13. See also Braaten and Jenson, *Union with Christ*, and McGrath, *Iustitia Dei*, 223–35.

However, it is dangerous to generalize from one example. It may be that the thief completed the process of sanctification through patiently enduring his torturous death on the cross. Moreover, this verse doesn't teach that the thief will be instantly perfected at the moment of death: the "today" of Christ's promise is consistent with a finite interval. In opposition to this, there is the passage in 1 Corinthians 3, in which Paul teaches that those who have built with straw will enter eternal life "as through fire" (v. 15), certainly suggesting something like a purgative process. (See section 4 below on purgatory.)

The Lutheran conception of glorification embodies a kind of Gnosticism, wrongly identifying our sinfulness with our physical bodies. Lutheran theologians assume that the death of our mortal bodies will, all by itself, free us forever from the propensity to sin, as though sin's reality in our lives is grounded entirely in our physical aspects. In fact, Paul uses the word "flesh" (*sarx*) to refer to aspects of our lives that are entirely mental, intellectual, and spiritual in nature (such as envy or pride).[14] If our soul is still "fleshly" at death, the mere separation of that soul from our bodies will not suffice to correct its disordered state: a process of purification after death will be required.

The Lutheran position depends on a strict distinction between justification (a change in status) and sanctification (a gradual, internal change). However, Lutherans read this distinction into, rather than out of, the Scriptures. In many places, the words *sanctify* and *renew* are used interchangeably with *justify* and *save*. Consider for example: Acts 26:17–18; 1 Corinthians 6:11; 2 Thessalonians 2:13; Hebrews 10:10, 13–14; 13:12; 1 Peter 1:1–2 (see Appendix B).

Grace as favor vs. grace as gift

Lutherans insist that the grace by which we are saved is the undeserved favor of God, granted to us for Christ's sake, while Roman

---

14. Romans 7:25; 8:1–13; Galatians 3:3; 5:16–25; 6:8.

A Lutheran's Case for Roman Catholicism

Catholics insist that grace is primarily a gift: the gift of the Holy Spirit, and of the "habitual grace" that the Spirit produces in the believer's life, especially the supernatural virtues of faith, hope, and love.

The word *grace* (*charis*) in the New Testament seems to carry both meanings:

- Meaning favor: Romans 3:24; 4:4; 5:20, 21; 6:1, 14, 15; 11: 5, 6; Galatians 1:6; 2:21; Ephesians 1:7; 2:7–8; 2 Thessalonians 2:16; 2 Timothy 1:9; Titus 3:7; 1 Peter 1:13; 2:20; Jude 1:4.

- Meaning help: Acts 14:26; 20:32; Romans 1:5; 12:3, 6; 2 Corinthians 1:15; 8:4, 6–7; 12:9; Galatians 2:9; Ephesians 3:8; 4:7, 29; 2 Timothy 2:1; Hebrews 4:16; 12:15; 13:9; James 4:6; 1 Peter 4:10; 5:5; 2 Peter 3:18.

Thus, the repeated emphasis in Paul's letters that we are "saved by grace" does not clearly support the Lutheran position.

Faith, not works

In addition, Lutherans appeal to Paul's teaching that there is a contradiction between being saved by faith and being saved by works of the Law. The main problem here is that Luther's interpretation seems to involve an extrapolation from the text. The "work of the Law" that Paul most clearly has in mind is circumcision, an external sign required by the old covenant. Read strictly, Paul is saying that we are not justified by any works of the Torah (the law of the Sinai covenant), including (but not limited to) works related to the ceremonial aspects of that Law. Luther extrapolates this Pauline doctrine to exclude any human actions whatsoever. As N. T. Wright has argued,[15] Paul's central concern, throughout Romans 3 and 4 and the book of Galatians, is to secure the equality of Jews and Gentiles by insisting that fulfilling the law of Moses, which effected the complete separation of the Jews from the Gentile world

---

15 Wright, *What St. Paul Really Said.* See also Sanders, *Paul and Palestinian Judaism,* and Dunn, *The New Perspective on Paul.*

through circumcision and the kosher regulations, is not in any sense a prerequisite for introduction into the grace of Christ (see Romans 3:28-31; Galatians 3:17).

The standard Lutheran response[16] is to point to Romans 7:7, in which the commandment against coveting is given as an example of what the Law demands. This is certainly a moral, and not merely a ceremonial or ritual, requirement. Here, Lutherans follow Augustine's interpretation of Paul and reject St. Jerome's suggestion that "work of the law" be limited to the ceremonial law of Sinai.

Lutherans and Roman Catholics agree that Augustine, and not Jerome, has the better interpretation. Paul certainly meant to include the moral law, and not merely the ceremonial law, in insisting that we are justified by faith, apart from the works of the Law. However, we must pay close attention to Paul's use of *work* and *law* in these passages. It is significant that Paul uses the word *work* (*ergon*) here. Paul consistently talks of the "works of the flesh" as opposed to the "fruit (*karpos*) of the Spirit" (see especially Galatians 5:19-23). A "work" of the Law would seem to be more than just acting in accordance with or fulfilling the Law. By associating "work" and "law" with "flesh" (Romans 3:20 and 8:3; Galatians 2:16 and 3:2-3), Paul seems to be defining a "work of the Law" as something that is

(1) an autonomous act of an independent self,

(2) natural,

(3) entirely under one's own exclusive control,

(4) having a self-contained value, that is, it places God under an obligation to repay one (Romans 4:4),

(5) a value that is obvious and measurable in human terms, and

(6) a finite value, unable to compensate for the guilt of sin (and so entailing the necessity of perfect compliance with the law).

---

16 Found already in Melanchthon's *Apology*, for example (article II, Book of Concord, 39).

The fruit of the Spirit, in contrast, is

(1) wholly the work of God in us,

(2) supernatural in quality,

(3) a matter of cooperation between the individual and the Spirit,

(4) having a value that depends on its connection to Christ and his merits, with the result that any reward it receives is the result of a free promise, not a debt,

(5) a value that is hidden and mysterious, beyond human judgment, and

(6) a value that is infinite, overwhelming, and negating the guilt of our daily sins.

This distinction corresponds roughly, but not perfectly, to a temporal distinction: before and after conversion. All of our attempts to justify ourselves prior to conversion to Christ will fall into the first category, works of the law. In general, the good we do after conversion, when moved by the Holy Spirit and regenerated by Christ's own life, will fall into the second category. However, as Paul's Epistle to the Galatians demonstrates, it is possible for Christians to fall back into a purely law-based system, seeking to replace self-effort and the letter of the law for God's grace and the leading of the Spirit.

Roman Catholics interpret these passages as teaching that we are justified, not by our outward actions, but by the fruit of the Spirit, including the inner quality of our heart (which is certainly a theme of Jesus and of the later prophets). Moreover, this inner quality is not something we have created ourselves—it is a free gift infused into us by God's grace for Christ's sake. In addition, the quality and its value cannot be separated from Christ and his merits: the inner quality is the very life of Christ within us, and the quality merits salvation only by uniting us to Christ and his merits, not by virtue of any natural or intrinsic power or virtue in them. This inner quality is, in the first instance, the virtue of faith, but it also encompasses hope (trust) and love or charity. As Paul himself teaches, we are justified by "faith working through love" (Galatians 5:6).

The crucial question is: should Paul's use of "works" and "works of the law" in Romans and Galatians be given a wide (Lutheran) or narrow (Roman Catholic) interpretation? There are several reasons for the narrower reading. First, an argument from silence. In contrast to Paul's descriptions of the fruit of the Spirit, he never describes these works (in Romans 3 and 4; Galatians 3) as connected to Christ or to the working of the Spirit within us. Second, in both contexts, Paul's wider argumentative strategy is to establish that Christ's death is necessary for our salvation and that faith in Christ equalizes the Jew and the Gentile. Paul's arguments in these passages successfully carry out this strategy under the narrower reading. Even if the fruit of the Spirit of Christ is needed for justification, this would in no way negate the absolute necessity of Christ's death and our rebirth through faith. Third, the narrower reading is required to make these passages consistent with the many scriptural passages that teach that judgment is according to works, that eternal life is a reward, that works justify (James 2:24), and that we should be zealous to confirm our calling and election (2 Peter 1:10). Finally, the Church Fathers for the first 1,500 years consistently take the narrower reading for granted (for example, see Augustine's view of justification expounded in Appendix C).

As many modern scholars have observed, Luther's anxiety about his own worthiness for salvation is remote from Paul's concerns in these passages. Luther required the wider reading of "works" in order to use these Pauline texts to resolve his own existential crisis, and subsequent Lutherans have treated these texts, understood in this way, as the hermeneutic key to understanding the rest of the Scriptures. However, this theological method is fundamentally unsound, a violation of the correct principle of letting Scripture interpret Scripture. Romans 3 and 4 needs to be interpreted in light of the rest of Scripture, just as much as other passages need to be interpreted in light of Romans 3 and 4. To privilege one small part of the whole canon and to apply the

Scripture-interprets-Scripture principle in one direction only is arbitrary and an invitation to error and distortion.

Next, let's consider Paul's use of "law," given the historical context (namely, the conflict with Judaizers over circumcision). By "work of the Law," Paul could mean a work that is part of a way of life that aims at the fulfillment of the law of Sinai, *taken as a whole*, including both ceremonial and moral aspects. What Paul is centrally concerned with denying is that works of the Law in that sense are necessary for salvation. If they were, then the law of Sinai would have had a salvation-conveying intention and function. This would make Christ's life, death, and resurrection superfluous. In fact, Paul argues, the law of Sinai was never intended to save anyone. This is not to deny that those human actions that are fruits of the Spirit, performed as a result of Christ living in us, might have some salvific significance. These are simply not "works of the Law" in the relevant sense.

The strongest argument for the Lutheran position is based on those passages in which Paul connects justification through faith and not through works with salvation by grace. If we were justified at all by works, we could not be saved by grace: Romans 3:24, 28; 4:4; 11:6, 2 Timothy 1:9. This seems to suggest that faith is pure receptivity, that faith as such in no way merits salvation, so our being saved through faith is in no conflict with our being saved for no merit of our own.

Is there a plausible Catholic interpretation of these passages? I think so. Again, bear in mind that the paradigmatic *work* for Paul is circumcision. If we could be justified before God by performing such rituals, grace would indeed be unnecessary. A human being, no matter how sinful, no matter how lacking in the Spirit-given inner qualities of faith, hope, and love, could live a life in outward conformity to the rituals and external requirements of the law of Moses, as Paul himself did before his conversion. Those works do not suffice—we need the infusion of God's grace to enable us to become, on the inside, the sort of person acceptable to God. (Again, this echoes themes in the teaching of Jesus, James, and the prophets.) The autonomous actions of a human being burdened by original sin, and intended to place God under a legal obligation, cannot justify. In fact, this is exactly Augustine's interpretation of Paul (as expressed, for example, in *On the Spirit and the Letter*—see Appendix C).

The Lutheran interpretation of the Pauline passages on faith versus works has the advantage of being simpler than the hypothesis that "works of the law" refers to the system of Sinai as a whole. Lutherans postulate that Paul is saying essentially the same thing in Romans 3 and 4; Galatians; Ephesians 2; 2 Timothy 1; and Titus 3: in each case, Paul is excluding every kind of work, both before and after conversion, both according to the law of Moses and according to natural law, from playing any role in our justification. On my alternative interpretation, these passages have to be divided into those that exclude the relevance of any pre-conversion works to the receiving the grace of first justification (Ephesians 2; 2 Timothy 1; and Titus 3) and those that exclude the necessity of observing the law of Moses, both before and after conversion, since salvation is by Christ, and the ceremonial and ritual aspects of the Law are merely shadows and tutors whose job is now completed (Romans 3 and 4; Galatians 2 and 3; Philippians 3). My view has to give significantly different readings to phrases that seem quite similar: "not by works," "not because of deeds done by us in righteousness," "not in virtue of our works" (Ephesians 2:9; Titus 3:5; 2 Timothy 1:9, meaning apart from all pre-conversion works under the moral law), in contrast to: "apart from law," "justified by works," "righteousness apart from works," "not justified by works of the law," "not justified before God by the law," "not having a righteousness of my own, based on the law" (Romans 3:21; 4:2 and 4:6; Galatians 2:16; 3:11; Philippians 3:9, meaning works of the Law of Sinai). Most difficult for my interpretation is Romans 4:4–6, where Paul's use of "works" has to be interpreted as referring to works as defined by the law of Moses (including circumcision), despite the fact that Paul does not use the phrase "works of the law," bringing his wording very close to those passages, like Ephesians 2:9, where "works" clearly refers to any supposedly meritorious action prior to the reception of grace.

Three things can be said in response. One is that simplicity is an advantage, but not a decisive advantage. One must also consider the immediate context within which each of Paul's use of "works" or "law" occurs. Where Paul is concerned to emphasize the fact that salvation in Christ breaks down the ethnic barrier between Jews and Gentiles (as in Romans 4, Galatians, and Philippians 3), it is natural to read "works" throughout as referring to observing the law of Moses. Where Paul is emphasizing the graciousness of God's gift to everyone, Jew and Gentile alike, a broader reading of "works" is appropriate.

Second, the Lutheran interpretation does not in fact deliver a perfectly simple explanation of Paul's words. In the Epistle to the Galatians, Paul is attempting to prove that Gentile Christians are not under any obligation at all to take on the whole legal system of Sinai, including circumcision. He does not deny, however, that Gentile Christians are under a real obligation to love, to avoid coveting and adultery, etc. If Paul were merely arguing that "works of the law" are not the basis for our justification, then Paul's "Judiaizing" opponents could have responded that circumcision remained necessary as an expression of our faith, just as works of charity are necessary. In Galatians (and in Romans 2–4), where Paul's point is the equalization of Jews and Gentiles, Paul's target must be the erroneous opinion that the law of Moses is necessary for salvation.

Third, as I have argued above, the two readings of "works" are not entirely unrelated, and so it is not surprising if, in passages like Romans 3 and 4, Paul brings the two together. If God had intended for the Law of Moses to be the means of the salvation of individuals, then Christ's death, and the grace that is available through Christ, would have been unnecessary. Autonomous, sinful persons (like the Paul before his conversion) are capable of external conformity to such a legal system. Conversely, if salvation were not a free and unmerited gift through faith in Christ, but were something sinful men could have earned, then observing the law of Moses would have had salvific significance before Christ's advent, and, therefore, would have continued in full force afterward, resulting in the continued division of Jews and Gentiles. Even when the two principles are brought together in this way, they do not entail, even jointly, that all works of the Christian, even works of love subsequent to conversion and empowered by God's grace, are irrelevant to his ultimate salvation. It is possible for a Christian to relapse into a purely law-based system of justification, relying upon his works, in their natural and visible aspects, apart from grace, to place God under an obligation to reward us. Paul saw the Galatians' embracing of universal circumcision as symptomatic of such a relapse.

Lutherans reject the Roman Catholic teaching that we are justified by infused faith, hope, and love on the grounds that love is a kind of work, excluded by Paul's teaching. However, isn't faith (in the sense of active trust) itself a kind of work? Moreover, isn't it the case that trusting in Christ (saving faith, in the Lutheran sense) must include hoping in God and loving God (as he is revealed in Christ)? I don't just mean that love is a necessary consequence of saving faith, but that hope and love are part and parcel of a saving faith. To trust someone is to love them: perhaps not perfectly, but at least to some degree. If we remember that "faith" for Rome is defined simply as intellectual assent to the doctrines of revelation, then it is plausible that faith in the Lutheran sense includes all three of faith, hope, and love in the Roman sense (at least to a rudimentary degree). For Roman Catholics, love is primarily a virtue of the will, while Lutherans insist that faith must involve the will as well as the intellect. Moreover, Lutherans will agree that there is something absurd about supposing that someone has a saving faith in Christ while thoroughly hating him. I'm not denying that there is a real distinction between trust and love, but only that the former includes an element of the latter.

Lutherans insist that we are saved by faith alone because we are, even after regeneration, unable to keep the Law perfectly. The Law's primary function is as a mirror, revealing to us our sinfulness and our need for a Savior. The Roman Church does not deny that believers stand in daily need of forgiveness through the merits of Christ. Our works that merit eternal life "fulfill" the Law (Romans 8:4), not by achieving a perfect, unbroken conformity to the Law's requirements, but by being the fruit of the Spirit—the result of the supernatural renewal of our lives in Christ, connecting us to Christ, who alone perfectly fulfilled the Law's demands. Both sides agree that there is a forensic aspect to justification, one that renders perfect conformity to the law unnecessary for salvation.

The weakness of the Lutheran position lies in its one-sidedness. Even in the texts most central to Lutheran theology (the Epistles to the Romans and the Galatians), there are many passages that indicate that our renewed life in the Spirit is essential to salvation:

- God will give eternal life "to those who by patience in well-doing seek for glory and immortality" (Romans 2:7).
- "Glory and honor and peace for everyone who does good . . . For God shows no partiality" (Romans 2:10–11).
- "Since we are justified by faith . . . we have obtained access to this grace in which we stand" (Romans 5:1–2).
- "If by the Spirit you put to death the deeds of the body you will live" (Romans 8:13).
- "The one who sows to the Spirit will from the Spirit reap eternal life" (Galatians 6:8).

Faith as "passive" and "merely receptive"

Lutheran theology includes the claim that we are in the reception of faith "purely passive," without any prior mode of activity (*modus agendi*).[17] This is obviously an attempt to maintain the consistency between the claim that we are justified solely by grace, without any dependence on any contribution from us, and the claim that only believers are justified in fact. If faith is a subjective condition of justification, how can it be claimed that we make no contribution? Only by denying that in believing we contribute anything to our justification: faith is merely the means by which we receive God's contribution.

---

17. Formula of Concord, Thorough Declaration, II, Book of Concord, 243, 247, 249–50.

However, it is not at all clear what could be meant by saying that faith is a state of pure passivity and receptivity. If it means that faith is a gift of God, that we are unable to believe by exercising our unaided capacity, then by the same token hope and love, and even the works that flow from a regenerate heart, could be described as purely passive and receptive in nature. Consider: "God's love has been poured into our hearts through the Holy Spirit" (Romans 5:5). What could be more passive than that?

Robert Preus argues that the verb "to believe" is, grammatically speaking, a verb expressing a mere state of being and not an action.[18] This is true, to the extent that the verb expresses a knowledge-like condition. To know that Christ died for our sins is simply to be in a certain condition; it is not a matter of *doing* anything. However, Preus here has forgotten that saving faith is not merely a matter of historical knowledge: it involves elements of assent and trust. To trust someone is to do something. The verb "to trust" is, grammatically speaking, a genuine action verb. Hence, saving faith is not merely passive, if this is supposed to correspond to a complete absence of action on the believer's part. Moreover, it is disingenuous for Lutherans to claim that this action of trust in God's promises is morally neutral: to refuse to trust in God is to violate the First Commandment, implicitly blaspheming by calling God a liar.

Lutherans insist that faith is a mere organ by which we receive Christ's righteousness. This begs the question: why must this organ of receptivity be identified with faith alone, and not with "faith working in love," or even with faith, regeneration, and the fruit that naturally flows from these? For example, Robert Preus writes, "If justification is declared freely (*dorean, gratis*) over the sinner by God's grace (Romans 3:24), then only faith is left to justify."[19] This is a non sequitur. If justification is free, how can anything be "left to justify"? If faith can justify despite our being justified "freely," then why is it impossible that it is faith and love together that do the justifying, so long as both are free gifts of God for Christ's sake?

---

18. Preus, *Justification and Rome*, 137–38 (footnote 103).
19. Preus, *Justification and Rome*, 97.

A Lutheran's Case for Roman Catholicism

As long as Rome is willing to admit (as it does) that our righteousness in Christ is an extrinsic matter, a matter of our being united to Christ and his righteousness, then the subjective basis of justification within us could be any condition that results from our union with Christ. There is no reason given why only faith could play this receptive role.

Lutherans sometimes put the issue this way: Roman Catholics teach that faith itself is a "virtue," while Lutherans deny this. Thus, Lutherans deny that we are justified by or through any of our virtues. In fact, Lutherans typically reject the very concept of a virtue as an unbiblical importation from Greek philosophy.[20] By asserting that we are justified in part through our virtues, Rome denies the doctrine of grace alone.

Once again, I think this argument is based on a terminological confusion. Preus, for example, describes a "virtue" as a "good work." This is not in fact the Roman Catholic definition, nor does it accord with the origins of the term in the philosophy of Plato and Aristotle. For Plato and Aristotle, a thing's *virtue* (*arête*) is that by which a thing is able to perform its natural function excellently. Good vision, for example, is a virtue of the eye, despite the fact that no one would think that having good vision was any kind of good work. The sharpness and hardness of its blade are virtues of a knife. Is faith a virtue, in this sense? Does God intend for the human mind and heart to know and to trust him? Certainly he does. Therefore, faith is, in the philosophical sense, a virtue of the soul. It is that by which the soul performs a vitally important function with respect to God and his promises.

Preus's mistake, and the mistake of many Lutheran theologians, is to confuse virtue with *natural moral* virtue. Even a moral virtue is not, strictly speaking, a good work, but it is an aspect of character by which a person is enabled to perform morally good works. Roman Catholic theologians (following Aquinas) do not describe faith as a moral virtue: it is instead, along with hope and love, a "supernatural" virtue. It is so called precisely because it is impossible for the natural man to believe (or to hope or to love)

---

20. Preus, *Justification and Rome*, 82.

without the assistance of God's grace. There is no reason why faith (and hope and love) could not be correctly described as both a virtue and a receiving organ of God's grace.

The no-boasting argument

Paul clearly teaches that being saved by grace excludes the possibility of human boasting (Romans 3:27; Ephesians 2:9). Lutherans take this to show that our salvation cannot be based on any internal quality or dependent on any cooperation on our part, since, if it did, we would have a basis for boasting.[21] This argument seems a non sequitur: so long as the internal qualities in question are gifts from God, so long as our cooperation is itself a fruit of God's grace, and so long as we must rely daily on God's mercy in Christ for the forgiveness of sins, any plausible basis for human boasting has been effectively excluded. As the new Catechism of the Catholic Church puts it, "the saints have always had a lively awareness that their merits were pure grace"[22] (paragraph 2011).

The distinction between Law and Gospel

Lutherans argue that Rome errs by confusing gospel and law. Gospel is promise, while law is demand. However, the promise of the gospel is not unconditional (unless we embrace universalism). The gospel says: you will be saved if (you believe, you repent and are baptized, you persevere until the end, etc.). Thus, the gospel can appropriately be described as a new law (the law of the Spirit, Romans 8; the law of liberty, James 1:25), consisting, as did the Torah, of a conditional promise.

When Roman Catholics describe the gospel as a "New Law," this could be no more controversial than describing it as a "New

21. See for example the Thorough Declaration of the Formula of Concord, III, Book of Concord, 30, on the purpose of the doctrine of justification by faith alone: "To afford saddened consciences dependable and reliable comfort, and *to give due honor* to the merit of Christ and the grace of God."

22. Catechism of the Catholic Church, 487.

Testament" or "New Covenant," since the Greek word *nomos* can certainly bear such a variety of meanings.

The word *gospel* means *the good news*. Hence, to argue that there is a deep and fundamental distinction between law and gospel is to presuppose that the law is not good news—i.e., that it is altogether bad news. This made sense so long as Lutherans affirmed that the law had only two uses: (i) as a curb and restraint on the actions of the wicked, and (ii) as a mirror and rule that reveals to us our inveterate sinfulness. Both of these uses do indeed deliver a kind of bad news to the sinner. However, Lutheran thought eventually (in the Formula of Concord) recognized a "third use of the law": as a guide to the believer, enabling the believer to live a wholesome and God-pleasing life. In its third use, the law does not deliver any bad news and so cannot be wholly separated from the gospel. The law in its third use could be seen as one of the blessings of the gospel won for us by Christ's life, death, and resurrection.

It cannot be denied that Christ did indeed act, in part, as a legislator. He tells us explicitly that his commandment that we should love one another as he has loved us is "a new commandment" (John 13:34).

Nonetheless, the Lutheran concern here is a legitimate one. There is always a danger of the Church's turning the New Covenant back into a version of the Old Covenant, through obsessive attention to external observances and legal standards. It is especially troubling when the Church invents new regulations by which it binds the consciences of its members. For example, the Roman Church imposes holy days of obligation, prescribes periods and forms of fasting, and requires periodic use of the sacraments of communion and penance. Isn't this exactly the kind of reliance of physical rituals that the prophets, Jesus, and Paul so earnestly warned us against?

There are, however, important differences between the rituals of the Old Covenant and the sacraments and precepts of the New. First, the sacraments are associated with God's promise of grace through union with Christ. They are not merely external observances, since God's promises invest them with a power to influence the heart and mind. They are not merely shadows of a redemption to come, but channels through which that redemption reaches the faithful. Second, the "precepts" of the Church do not define an all-encompassing form of physical life that separates God's people within from the Gentiles without by the meticulous regulation of diet, clothing, work, and shelter. The precepts are easily satisfied and compatible with Christian liberty of a wide scope. Thirdly, the precepts are not presented as on a par with God's eternal law (i.e., the Ten Commandments). Rather, this making of precepts is a matter of the Church's seeking that things should be done "decently and in good order" under the contingent conditions of contemporary culture. They are, therefore, similar to the regulations concerning the eating of blood and of food offered to idols adopted by the Church in Acts 15.

In *The Proper Distinction between Law and Gospel*, the American Lutheran theologian C. F. W. Walther makes a strong case for the practical, pastoral necessity of distinguishing between the law and gospel.[23] It is bad practice to preach the demands of the law to a broken-hearted, penitent sinner who is in danger of despair. To such a sinner, the greatness of God's mercy and the unlimited availability of God's grace for Christ's sake must be clearly presented. Conversely, to preach the free availability of God's grace to one in a state of obdurate and impenitent mortal sin is to miss an opportunity to move him to repentance, and the preaching of the good news of God's grace to the self-righteous man falls upon his deaf ears. No good Roman Catholic priest would deny the truth or importance of any of this. If Lutheran theology is taken to be entirely pastoral and kerygmatic in nature, then it is fully compatible with the systematic theology of Trent.

The error of the Lutheran systematic theologian is to suppose that it is possible to construct a theological system that cannot be misused or misapplied in pastoral practice. In fact, Walther himself recognized that this was not so: in addition to an understanding of the abstract propositions of Lutheran soteriology, it is also necessary to be instructed, by means of concrete examples and situated

23 Walther, *The Proper Distinction between Law and Gospel*.

guidelines, in the proper use of both law and gospel. In fact, Roman Catholic doctrine is just as compatible with good pastoral practice. Even though we are justified by infused righteousness, the penitent sinner needs to be reassured of God's unconditional favor, anchored in the merit of Christ, and even though God's grace is abundantly available, the complacent believer needs to be stimulated to diligence in good works.

Solo Christo: justified by Christ's righteousness alone

Luther's doctrine of salvation was thoroughly christocentric: this was its greatest virtue. The righteousness by which we are justified is the very righteousness of Christ, displayed in his life, sufferings and death, and resurrection: see Galatians 2:20; 1 Corinthians 1:30; 2 Corinthians 5:21; and Philippians 3:9. In apparent contrast, the Council of Trent (Sixth Session) insisted that Christ's righteousness is the "meritorious" cause of our justification, but not the "formal" cause. The formal cause of our justification is the infused righteousness that we receive by grace (the infused virtues of faith, hope, and love).

There is certainly a difference of emphasis here, and Luther's christocentricity is a clear point in his favor. However, I am unconvinced that the position of Trent is really a heretical error, a denial of the essence of the gospel. By asserting that Christ's righteousness is the one and only meritorious cause of our justification, Trent seems to affirm that the merit of Christ's own righteousness is applied to us, making us proper objects of God's saving activity. In other words, there would seem to be perfect agreement about the basis of what Lutherans call our "objective" or "universal" justification. We merit the propitiation of God and the forgiveness of our sins solely by the merits of Christ himself.[24] The difference lies

---

24. The sufficiency of Christ's merits for objective justification is quite clear in the Catechism of the Catholic Church, especially paragraphs 615-17 and 1992. In paragraph 1451 (pp. 364-5 in the 1994 English translation), the Catechism states that the satisfaction that we make for our sins "help configure us to Christ, who alone expiated our sins once for all . . . [A]ll our boasting

on the issue of "subjective" or "personal" justification: what must happen to each of us individually for this objective justification to work for our eternal benefit.

Simultaneously saint and sinner

Rome does not claim that God's grace renders anyone sinless in this life: everyone sins daily and is in daily need of forgiveness for Christ's sake. At the same time, the Lutherans do not deny that there is something internal to us (*in nobis*) that is required for our justification: namely, the faith that lays hold of Christ's righteousness. So, the question comes down to this: what internal condition (*in nobis*) is required for us to lay hold of Christ's righteousness? The Scriptures sometimes speak of faith justifying or saving (or even of baptism as saving). These are understood as elliptical, expressing that it is Christ as believed in who justifies, or Christ in whom we are baptized who saves. By the same token, when Rome speaks of our being justified "by good works," this can be taken as also containing an ellipsis: we are justified by Christ as the one who brings forth good works in us as his fruit.

Lutherans say that it is faith alone that does the apprehending, although saving faith is always accompanied by regeneration and good works. Rome teaches that it is "faith working in love" that apprehends Christ's merits: that is, that is the whole process, including both faith (as its root) and hope, love, and works of charity (as the fruit), that is involved in apprehending Christ. In both cases, it is only Christ and only his merits that reconcile us to God. Lutherans are unfair in claiming that the Romans propose to *substitute* our merits for Christ's. One could, with as much justice, claim that Lutherans propose to "substitute" our faith for Christ's merits. The biblical evidence (including the Lutheran's most important text, Romans 4), simply doesn't, taken as a whole, clearly favor the Lutheran position.

---

is in Christ, in whom we make satisfaction by bringing forth 'fruits that befit repentance.' These fruits have their efficacy from him, by him they are offered to the Father, and through him they are accepted by the Father."

Meriting an increase in grace (unmerited favor) is a self-contradiction

On the Roman view, by cooperating with God's grace, we can "merit" a further increase in that grace. This seems to be a flat-out self-contradiction: how can we merit an increase in unmerited help? If help is provided on the basis of merit, then it is not by grace.

The Roman language of "merit" certainly lends itself to confusion here. Roman theologians distinguish two kinds of "merit": condign and congruous. There is, theoretically, a third kind of merit, which I will call "absolute" or "strict" merit. "Absolute" merit would be the kind of righteousness that would compel God, by virtue of strict justice and apart from any economy of gracious promises, to accept us as worthy of eternal life. Roman theologians, following Aquinas, simply deny that human creatures can claim any such absolute merit (see the Catechism of the Catholic Church, paragraph 2007, p. 486). As absolutely sovereign, God cannot be bound in strict justice to any of his creatures: so no one can claim absolute merit before God. For this reason, they do not speak of our "earning" our salvation, and they can agree with Paul that salvation cannot be thought of as wages earned by work done: "to one who works, his wages are not reckoned as a gift, but as his due" (Romans 4:4).

Condign merit presupposes the order of grace but implies, within that order, a kind of fit between the quality possessed or the work done and the reward received, due to God's explicit promise. *Congruous* merit refers to a kind of value that God freely chooses to reward, apart from any promise to do so. (In fact, different Roman theologians have drawn this distinction differently, but I think that, in the final analysis, the distinction has little to do with the issue at hand.)

Correcting the errors of some of the nominalists (like Ockham and Biel) to whom the Reformers had rightly objected, the Council of Trent clearly denied that human beings are able to merit, either condignly or congruously, their own conversion to faith (the so-called "first justification").[25] According to Trent, we are able (after regeneration) to merit further increases in grace, and ultimately eternal life itself, condignly. However, the equality between merit and reward depends ultimately on the fact that we are cooperating with God's own grace, so that "it is no longer I who live, but Christ who lives in me" (Galatians 2:20). As Augustine put it, God is simply crowning his own gifts to us.

For Aquinas and scholastic theologians in general, "merit" comes to have a primarily causal, rather than judicial, meaning. That is, a condition "merits" an increase in grace just in case it satisfies a causally necessary precondition for that increase in grace. Understood in this way, the Thomistic concept of merit approximates the Lutheran notion of a "means of grace." For Lutherans, there are activities that we can participate in (namely, baptism, hearing and reading the Word, holy communion, confession and absolution) by which we have access to God's grace. In Thomistic terms, these activities "merit" an increase in grace, not in the sense that the grace is earned or deserved by them, but simply in the sense that God has promised to reward them with an increase in grace. This is not to deny that there is a difference between the two perspectives at this point: first, the different understandings of "grace" (forgiveness and imputed righteousness only, versus regeneration and the infusion of Christ's righteousness), and, second, a difference in the scope of activities that "merit" or serve as "means" of grace (the Catholic view including many things, like prayer and almsgiving, that Lutherans would exclude).

---

25. ". . . we are therefore said to be justified freely, because none of those things which precede justification—whether faith or works—merit the grace itself of justification" (Council of Trent, Sixth Session, chapter VIII). See also the Catechism, paragraph 2010, p. 487: "No one can merit the initial grace of forgiveness and justification."

Post-Vatican II Neo-Pelagianism: salvation through other religions

The documents of Vatican II seem to hold out the hope that some may be saved through a kind of "prevenient" grace available in non-Christian religions. Since this can't be through explicit faith in Christ, it must be by human works alone. This would seem to commit Vatican II to the error of Pelagius, according to which the grace and mercy available in Christ are not strictly necessary for salvation.

Here again, however, the Roman Catholic position can be defended by emphasizing that, in every case, the objective basis of justification is the life and death of Christ alone. The issue in dispute concerns subjective justification: to attain the benefits of Christ's righteousness, must one be baptized and embrace a faith that explicitly names Christ as its object? The problem with such a strict exclusivity is that of accounting for the salvation of the many Old Testament saints, such as Adam, Noah, or Job, who seem to have had only a very minimal knowledge of the Savior who was to come. Could not such an inchoate knowledge of Christ as Savior be the basis for a saving trust in God among contemporary non-Christians who, through a simple lack of opportunity, have never heard the gospel?

The motivation for good works

Some Protestants have criticized the Roman position for encouraging a purely mercenary motivation for good works. In contrast, the Lutheran teaches that our only motivation for good works should be our love and gratitude toward God, in response to his free gift of salvation in Christ. The Lutheran reformers argued, rightly I think, that the doctrine of justification through faith alone would not open the floodgates of licentiousness. Gratitude is indeed a powerful motivation.

However, the Roman position does not entail that our only reason for good works is as a means to our own salvation. The existence of a lower motivation (the fear of hell or the desire for heaven) does not exclude the operation of a higher motivation (disinterested love of God). As sinful people, we should welcome any motive force that can keep us from the entangling grip of sin.

Moreover, given the possibility of losing one's salvation, Lutherans too can be motivated to avoid sin by the possibility of hell. A life of carnality can lead to unrepentance and unbelief, ending in apostasy (2 Peter 1:10).

Doesn't the Roman position, however, lead either to a mercenary, calculating attitude toward our own works, or to perpetual insecurity about whether we have done enough to satisfy God's standards? If the Roman teaching is properly understood, neither of these consequences follows. The supernatural quality by which our works merit eternal life is knowable only to God himself. We cannot discern this quality by examining either the outward expression of our works or the inner workings of our conscious minds. In the end, we must simply trust in God's grace and mercy for Christ's sake, confident that God will produce through us such works and will for Christ's sake accept and reward them. Luther's important rediscovery of our need to look to Christ, outside of us, and not to look obsessively within ourselves, is entirely consistent with the teaching of the Council of Trent that our works have a role to play, both in meriting eternal life and in sustaining us in a state of grace.

The case for the Roman Catholic side

Salvation as a reward

Lutherans claim that the idea of human merit (apart from the merits of Christ) is utterly alien to the Scriptures, yet the Bible often speaks of works as meriting eternal life: Revelation 20:12–15; Matthew 25:31–46; Romans 2:6, 9–11, and 8:13; Galatians 6:7–8; 2 Corinthians 5:10. These Scriptures do not merely teach that all who are saved (through their faith alone) also do good works, but that they are judged by the quality of the works they do. This can be reconciled with Paul's formula of "grace through faith, not works," by supposing that these good works are not merely external works in conformity to the ceremonial law, that the works count as meriting eternal life only for the sake of Christ's merits, and that the works are meritorious only because they are the fruits of the Holy Spirit at work within the believer. Moreover, these passages do not deny that the believers' sins are freely forgiven for Christ's sake.

The Scriptures also speak of eternal life as a reward: Colossians 3:24; Hebrews 10:35 and 11:6; Revelation 11:18 and 22:12; and as a prize: Philippians 3:14; 1 Corinthians 9:24; 2 Timothy 4:8; James 1:12.

The Lutheran Reformer Phillip Melanchthon, in his *Apology for the Augsburg Confession* (one of the official Lutheran confessions) discusses these passages in Article III. He claims that Rome teaches that good works "are worthy of grace and life eternal, and do not stand in need of mercy, or of Christ as mediator."[26] This is inaccurate, for two reasons. First, it overlooks the fact that believers rely on the forgiveness of sins, which is freely offered on a daily basis to believers[27] and, for more serious sins, in the sacrament of penance on the basis of Christ's merit alone. Second, it fails to take into account the fact that the works merit eternal life only because they are the fruit of God's work within us for Christ's sake.[28]

Melanchthon writes:

> We do not contend concerning the term "reward." We dispute concerning the matter, namely, whether good

---

26. Melanchthon, *Apology of the Augsburg Confession*, article III, p. 66.

27. "For, although, during this mortal life, men, how holy and just soever, at times fall into at least light and daily sins, which are also called venial, not therefore do they cease to be just. For that cry of the just, 'Forgive us our trespasses,' is both humble and true" (Trent, Sixth Session, chapter XIV). The distinction between mortal or grave sins and light or venial ones is taught explicitly in 1 John 5:16 (sins leading to death versus sins not so leading).

28. "Jesus Christ Himself continually infuses his virtue into the said justified—as the head into the members, and the vine into the branches—and this virtue always precedes and accompanies and follows their good works, which without it could not in any wise be pleasing and meritorious before God..." (Council of Trent, Sixth Session, chapter XVI).

> works are themselves worthy of grace and of eternal life, or whether they please only on account of faith, which apprehends Christ as mediator . . . If the adversaries will concede that we are accounted righteous by faith because of Christ, and that good works please God because of faith, we will not afterwards contend much concerning the term "reward." We confess that eternal life is a reward, because it is something due on account of the promise, not on account of our merits . . . Now if passages which treat of works are understood in such a manner as to comprise faith, they are not opposed to our doctrine . . . Therefore, it is a sufficient reason why eternal life is called a reward, because thereby the tribulations which we suffer, and the works of love which we do, are compensated, although we have not deserved it.[29]

Melanchthon seems here to be conceding, on behalf of the Lutheran Church, that it is not objectionable to speak of eternal life as a reward for our good works, so long as it is conceded that these good works are meritorious only because of our faith in Christ as the mediator. He later, in the same text, seems to admit that eternal life is a kind of "compensation" given to us for our good works and our suffering for Christ's sake: "Therefore it is a sufficient reason why eternal life is called a reward, because thereby the tribulations which we suffer, and the works of love which we do, are *compensated*, although we have not deserved it." If this is correct, these are devastating concessions on Melanchthon's part, since the Roman Church readily concedes the point Melanchthon insists on. Our works are meritorious only insofar as they are the fruit of Christ's work within us, a grace merited entirely by Christ's own death and passion. The Council of Trent stated that faith is the "root" and "foundation" of justification, without which it is impossible to please God (Hebrews 11:6) and to come into the fellowship of his sons (Council of Trent, Sixth Session, chapter VIII). Moreover, it asserts that works cannot justify apart from Christ as mediator, since "no one can be just, but he to whom the merits of the Passion

---

29. Melanchthon, *Apology of the Augsburg Confession*, III, Book of Concord, 67.

of our Lord Jesus Christ are communicated" (Council of Trent, Sixth Session, chapter VII).

Melanchthon's distinction between merit and what is due according to God's promise, displays a misunderstanding of what the Roman Church means by "merit." Since there can be no claims of strict justice on the part of creatures upon God, apart from his own gracious promises, Rome teaches that all of our virtues and works can "merit" God's blessing only by virtue of those blessings being due to us according to God's promise.

The fatal contradiction in the Lutheran position

Lutherans affirm what seem to be three mutually inconsistent theses: (1) that we can lose our faith, and thereby our salvation, (2) that our faith is strengthened through the external means of grace (Word and sacrament), which require our diligent use, and (3) that our works have absolutely no role in securing our final salvation. Calvinists and modern evangelicals who embrace the theory of "once saved, always saved," have the virtue of logical consistency. On their view, once we have received the free gift of salvation through faith, there is absolutely nothing we can do or fail to do that would entail the loss of our salvation. The Lutheran Confessions (the *Apology of the Augsburg Confession* and the Formula of Concord) rightly rejects this position as offering a merely "carnal assurance." For example, Melanchthon writes in the *Apology*:

> Peter teaches (II Peter 1:10) why good works should be done, namely, that we may make our calling sure, that is, that we may not fall from our calling if we again sin. "Do good works," he says, "that you may persevere in your heavenly calling, that you may not fall away again and lose the Spirit and the gifts, which came to you, not on account of the works that follow, but of grace, through Christ, and are now retained by faith. But faith does not remain in those who lead a sinful life, lose the Holy Spirit, and reject repentance."[30]

30. Melanchthon, *Apology of the Augsburg Confession*, Article XX, Book of Concord, 104.

The Question of Justification

Similarly, the Formula of Concord insists that grace can be lost through serious sin:

> [T]he false Epicurean delusion is to be earnestly censured and rejected, namely, that some imagine that faith and righteousness and salvation which they have received can be lost through no sins or wicked deeds, not even through willful and intentional ones, but that a Christian, although he indulges his wicked lusts without fear, resists the Holy Ghost, and purposely engages in sin against conscience, yet none the less retains faith, God's grace, righteousness and salvation.[31]

I won't here review the many scriptural passages (1 Corinthians 6:9; Galatians 5:21; Ephesians 5:4; Romans 8:13; Colossians 3:6, etc.) that seem to teach quite clearly that salvation depends on our perseverance in grace, which is incompatible with our living in serious, unrepentant sin, since this is common ground between Lutherans and Catholics.

There are two ways to make the Lutheran position consistent. First, a Lutheran might assert that our continuing in faith, and our avoidance of a kind of carnal sin that is incompatible with saving faith, has nothing whatsoever to do with our own efforts or our active cooperation with the Holy Spirit. This sort of quietism can be found in Luther, but it is explicitly rejected by later Lutheran dogmatists (as in the Formula of Concord, which insists that believers can and must cooperate with the Holy Spirit). Such quietism seems inconsistent with the many exhortations to avoid the occasions of sin and to remain faithful in worship and the study of the Scriptures to be found throughout the New Testament. All these exhortations would have to be taken as serving only to reveal to believers their continuing sinfulness (denying altogether what Lutherans describe as the third use of the law).

Alternatively, a Lutheran could admit that we can cooperate in our own sanctification but deny that progress in sanctification

---

31. Formula of Concord: Thorough Declaration, Book of Concord, section IV, p. 258. The Thorough Declaration is also commonly known in English as the "Solid Declaration."

has any effect on our persistence in saving faith. This not only flies in the face of common sense and Christian experience: it is also difficult to square with scriptural injunctions to avoid a fall into sin and unrepentance (1 Corinthians 10:12; Hebrews 3:12; 1 Peter 3:17).

Thus, it seems that Lutherans must admit that our works do contribute to our final salvation, so speaking of "salvation through faith alone" is an exaggeration.

A Lutheran might respond at this point with the charge that Roman theologians are excessively concerned with logical consistency. Salvation involves an element of impenetrable mystery, beyond human comprehension, and it is therefore improper to seek to reduce doctrine to a logically coherent system. This disqualification of logic cuts both ways, however. The core of the case for the Lutheran consists of the claim that Roman doctrines *contradict* the biblical principle of *sola gratia*. The identification of such a contradiction is a logical matter. A Roman theologian could respond, with considerable justice, that the Lutheran is overlooking the paradoxical relationship between divine grace and human freedom, expressed by Paul himself in the Epistle to the Philippians: "Work out your salvation with fear and trembling, for God is at work in you, both to will and to work for His good pleasure" (2:12–13). Lutheran theology attempts to reduce this paradox to a logical dilemma: either salvation through grace alone or salvation requiring an element of human cooperation, but not both.

Eternal vs. temporal penalties, penance, satisfaction, and indulgences

Roman theologians make a distinction between two kinds of penalty for sin, temporal and eternal. There are, correspondingly, two kinds of satisfaction to be made for our sins. The eternal penalty for our sins refers to the infinite weight of guilt, and the concomitant wrath of God, that accompanies all of our sins as acts of rebellion against God's reign. Complete satisfaction for this eternal penalty was made by Christ on the cross. The merits of the believer or of the saints can make no contribution to this finished work.

In addition to this eternal penalty and its satisfaction, Roman theologians teach that our post-baptismal sins also incur a temporal penalty that must be satisfied by acts of penance. This temporal satisfaction does not propitiate a wrathful God, nor does it in any way balance the scales of justice. These works are exclusively those of the cross of Christ. However, a loving God can and does discipline his children, even when they are redeemed and fully reconciled with him. God disciplines believers, out of love, not justice: 2 Samuel 12; 1 Corinthians 11:32; Hebrews 12:5–11; Revelation 3:19.

In addition, it is fitting that believers offer to God some penitential token after having displeased him, as a means of expressing their sorrow and remorse. Failure to do so can constitute a further sin of omission, failing to take seriously the demands of an ongoing friendship with God.

The Roman Church quite reasonably combined the satisfaction of the temporal penalties of sin with the Office of the Keys, the Lutheran term for the sacrament (or quasi-sacrament) by which the Church absolves sins. This rite is known in the West as Penance or Reconciliation. The penalties imposed in the sacrament of Penance are not conditions that must be met in order to earn forgiveness: the absolution of sins is given freely and unconditionally. (Any sin, no matter how serious, can be forgiven through the sacraments of baptism and penance.) The penalties are laid upon the believer subsequently, as an aid to sanctification and as a means to restoring fellowship with God.

The penitential system arose early in the Church in response to the periodic persecutions of the Roman Empire. When a wave of persecution abated, the Church had to deal with those believers who had escaped death by practicing idolatry and denying their faith. Rigorists demanded that such believers never be allowed to return to Church fellowship. The Church rejected such rigorism, insisting that God's forgiveness was still available to believers who had fallen, even when very serious sins were involved (idolatry, murder, adultery). The Church did insist, however, that such penitents accept temporary disciplines, as an expression of the sincerity of their sorrow and as a token to God and to their brethren of their recognition of the damage that their sin had done to the cause of the kingdom.

Roman Catholic theologians presumed that such ecclesiastical penalties, if unfulfilled in this life, would be carried out in a purgatorial state. Penalties that are imposed by the Church can be modified and lightened by the Church (in the form of "indulgences"). These indulgences do not literally shorten one's stay in purgatory by a specified number of days: they simply remit temporal, ecclesiastical penalties. This particular theory about the extension of ecclesiastical penalties into the afterlife has been a popular one among Roman Catholics until recently, but, as far as I know, it was never a matter of dogmatic definition. The new Catechism of the Catholic Church spends only four pages (out of over a thousand) on purgatory and offers only a very sketchy outline about the state. The emphasis now is on discipline as a means of purifying the soul (as trials refine our faith in this life—1 Peter 1:6–7), rather than on payment of ecclesiastical penalties. Indulgences are also discussed only briefly, with the explanation that it is possible, thanks to the intimate bond of the fellowship of the Spirit, to help souls in purgatory to bear the burdens of their purification.

There is no dispute, that at the time of the Reformation, the Church was obsessed with earning release from the temporal penalties and from purgatory. This did indeed obscure the teaching of grace and minimized the value of our redemption in Christ. This unhealthy preoccupation has not entirely disappeared, but it is greatly abated (in part due to reforms initiated already at Trent).

Lutherans object to the very idea of temporal penalties, especially when these are projected beyond death into a purgatorial state, on the grounds that this doctrine contradicts the sufficiency of Christ's sacrifice. If Christ's sacrifice is sufficient to pay for all of the eternal penalties of our sins, surely it must, a fortiori, be sufficient to pay for the lesser, temporal penalties. This objection overlooks the fact that eternal and temporal penalties are *penalties*

The Question of Justification

in radically different senses of the word. Eternal penalties are grounded in the fact that sinners are cut off from God's love and placed under his wrath and judgment. Temporal penalties are grounded in the fact that believers are under the care of a loving heavenly Father. Temporal penalties are sent by God to do us good, including the trials endured in purgatory. The souls in purgatory rejoice amidst their suffering, knowing that all that they endure comes directly from the loving hand of God. This is the answer to the common question of why the pope doesn't simply open the treasury of merit of the saints and free all the souls in purgatory with one stroke of the pen. When purgatorial trials are lessened by the actions of believers on earth, this does not occur because some account books in heaven have been rebalanced, but because the burdens of purification can (by the grace of God and through the fellowship of the Spirit) be shared, even across the chasm of death.

The notion of a "treasury of merits," in which the merits of Christ's life and passion are combined with those of Mary and the saints, and from which the Church draws in issuing indulgences to those performing specific works, is understandably a troubling one. How can Christ's merits be combined with those of the saints without diminishing the infinite value, and compromising the unique status, of Christ's death as our ransom and redemption? I think the answer to this worry involves distinguishing two kinds of merit associated with Christ's life and death. On the one hand, there is the infinite merit that Christ earned as the incarnate God, who gave up his life as a ransom for many. In this respect, Christ's merit is unique, all-sufficient, and incapable of being augmented in any way. On the other hand, Christ's life and death can be considered on a purely human plane, as the acts and sufferings of a member of the Church. On this plane, although unique in quality and quantity, Christ's merits are of a kind with our own and can be added to (as Paul teaches that the sufferings of the Church are filling what "is lacking" in Christ's suffering). The treasury of merits, in this sense, has nothing to do with ransoming us from sin, death, and the devil, or earning for us reconciliation and adoption into God's family. Rather, the treasury of merits is relevant only to healing the temporal wounds that result from post-baptismal sins, and to this task all believers can contribute (as we "bear one another's burdens").

The issues of self-righteousness and the assurance of salvation

Many Lutherans accuse the Roman doctrine as encouraging the sin of self-righteousness. In teaching that we merit eternal life by our works, the Roman Church seems to teach us to rely upon our own, autonomous efforts, as though we could, by choosing to live the right sort of life, place ourselves securely in a position of self-generated righteousness and spiritual superiority to others who are sinners. This charge ignores three things. First, the works that merit eternal life are themselves the fruit of grace, gifts of God's Spirit, and therefore not the product of the autonomous individual. Second, we cannot trust in our outward works, since the merit of any work depends on its supernatural quality as a fruit of the Holy Spirit. This supernatural quality is not under our control. In the end, we must place our faith wholly in the promise of the gift of the Spirit to us for Christ's sake. One cannot assess the merits of his own life in terms of the visible or introspectible character of one's deeds. Finally, the Roman Church insists that all believers sin daily and must rely on the forgiveness of their sins for Christ's sake.

Although Rome teaches that both love and good works play a role in justifying by uniting the believer with Christ, it does not teach that there is some specific level of the quality or quantity of one's good works that must be attained. The parable of the Late Workers is relevant here. God rewards our works without any reference to their intrinsic value, but for Christ's sake, in accordance with his own grace. We can rely confidently on God's grace and mercy, while simultaneously being busy with good works "to make our calling sure," as Peter describes it (2 Peter 1:10, KJV). One's life in Christ cannot be static: one is always either moving forward in sanctification or backsliding into the coldness of indifference and unbelief. As the Formula of Concord puts it, an "Epicurean" security that is indifferent to the dangers of sin is to be avoided. A wholesome fear of the consequences of spiritual sloth is quite consistent with a practical certainty in one's current standing in the state of grace, and with a confidence in the abundant availability of God's help and mercy.

Some Lutherans argue that the crux of the difference between Lutheranism and Rome lies in the question of the assurance of salvation. Although Roman theologians deny that the believer can be absolutely certain of their salvation, Catholics can have confidence in their own salvation, even a moral certainty, based on God's love and mercy and the abundance of grace available in the sacraments.

There is, in addition, a problem of terminology. When Lutherans speak of assurance of salvation, they mean the assurance that the believer is now in a state of grace, not the assurance that one will persevere until death. However, when Catholics deny the assurance of the salvation, it is primarily the latter that they have in mind. Since Lutherans agree with Catholics that we can lose our salvation (by losing our saving faith), the assurance of salvation that Lutheranism provides is a highly qualified one.

In fact, what Luther himself sought in the form of assurance was simply the belief that there was at least a bare *possibility* that he should persevere and be saved. For Luther, even this minimal assurance of the possibility of salvation depended on believing that his perseverance depended solely on God's sovereign election, and not at all on himself. This seems to rely on a non sequitur: namely, that if something is 100 percent God's work, then it is 0 percent ours. But Paul teaches that it can both ours and God's at once: "work out your salvation with fear and trembling, for it is God who is at work within you, both to will and to work" (Philippians 2:13).

There is one respect in which Lutheran assurance is decidedly inferior to its Roman counterpart. Lutherans deny that the sacraments (of baptism and of absolution/penance) are effective unless the individual exercises saving faith, while Romans stipulate that the sacraments are effective unless the individual actively intends to use them for base purposes. The technical term for this dispute is *ex opere operata* (Romans affirm this and Lutherans deny it).[32] The logical consequence of the Lutheran position is that I cannot be sure that I am now in a state of grace, reconciled to God, unless I am sure that I have saving faith. In contrast, the Catholic can be assured that his sins are forgiven, so long as he as not intentionally created some inner obstacle to the efficacy of the sacrament. This means that when the Catholic exercises faith or trust, the object of the trust is simply the grace and mercy of God, whereas when the Lutheran does so, he must to a certain degree rely on the quality of his own trust.[33]

This subjective, self-referential character of the Lutheran conception of trust can place a serious obstacle to one's assurance of one's present state of grace. To their credit, Lutheran theologians urge their laymen to direct their faith solely toward God's faithfulness as its object, but this instruction is inconsistent with the theory that the beneficial efficacy (although not the validity)[34] of the sacrament depends on the genuineness of the believer's faith.

32. The Lutheran position, however, is of doubtful consistency on this point, since Lutherans practice infant baptism. Granting for the sake of argument that it is possible for infants truly to believe, it is surely implausible that their belief precedes the operation of baptism in bestowing grace upon the child.

33. St. Paul warns against taking the Eucharist "unworthily," which Lutherans interpret as referring to the necessity of examining the genuineness of one's faith. Luther offers some concrete guidelines for the appropriate kind of self-examination in the Small Catechism. Lutherans don't trust in their own faith, but they must in practice rely on a self-assessment that is, at least potentially, problematic, due to its subjective orientation. The Catholic view of baptism and absolution, in contrast, places far greater focus on the efficacy of the objective, sacramental act, which results in forgiveness unless the subject introduces a positive obstacle (such as an ulterior intention or an unconfessed mortal sin).

34. Lutherans agree with Rome in rejecting the heresy of Donatism. Both agree that the validity of a sacrament depends in no way on the condition of either the minister or the recipient. A hypocrite receiving Holy Communion, for example, eats the body and drinks the blood of the Lord, just as much as a believer does. However, he eats and drinks to his own condemnation, not to his benefit. For Lutherans in particular, the sacrament delivers no benefit to the recipient unless received in genuine, saving faith. Here the Catholic view is more generous: so long as the recipient introduces no positive obstacle, the sacrament (e.g., absolution) delivers its benefit (forgiveness) effectively. This

The Question of Justification

George Lindbeck, a Protestant theologian who taught at Yale, has argued that Lutheran theology is most charitably interpreted as a metalinguistic or hermeneutic theory.[35] In other words, the Lutheran doctrine of justification should be seen as a set of rules about how to proclaim the grace-conveying promises of God, not as a quasi-scientific or metaphysical theory about how the Word and sacraments work. This doctrine prescribes that pastors and teachers proclaim the promises of the good news unconditionally to the penitent, in such a way that saving faith and regeneration transpires. "Your sins are forgiven," not "Your sins are forgiven, if you truly believe (or repent or live righteously hereafter)." This is a plausible view, but one that strips the status of truth (as opposed to pastoral utility) from Lutheran doctrine, making moot the question of whether truth lies with the Lutheran, as opposed to the Roman Catholic, teaching.

From the Lutheran perspective, the doctrine of the *ex opere operata* efficacy of sacramental absolution turns the Roman faith into a version of salvation through external works. By merely going through the motions of confession, moved only by the fear of hell and apart from faith in Christ, the penitent is made right with God. However, this objection overlooks the fact that, according to Roman teaching, the sacraments save by providing the grace that effects an internal transformation, the infusion of faith, hope, and love. If the penitent fails to cooperate with the Spirit in being united with Christ, the reconciliation made present by the sacrament of penance can do him no good in the final outcome. However, the proffered forgiveness and remission of sin are really conveyed by the sacrament and do not depend on the pre-existence of faith on the part of the recipient. Faith is the product of grace, not its precondition. In this way, the Roman position avoids the danger of an inward-looking subjectivism or pietistical self-righteousness.

---

difference puts the Lutheran in an awkward position vis-à-vis infant baptism. Lutherans must claim, without any evidence, that the infants of believing parents are themselves in a positive condition of saving faith.

35 Lindbeck, *The Nature of Doctrine*.

To be fair to Luther, many late scholastic and nominalist theologians, such as William of Ockham and Gabriel Biel, taught that, in order to enter a state of grace, one must first do one's very best or do "what lies within us." This well-intended but misconceived doctrine did engender horrible anxiety in many, Luther included, since one could never be sure that one had really done one's best. These opinions were aberrant within the Catholic tradition: nothing of the kind is found in Thomas Aquinas, who insists that there is nothing we need or can do prior to regeneration by the Spirit through the sacraments. Aquinas's position was explicitly affirmed by the Council of Trent.

In summary: the crux of the matter

Martin Chemnitz, the leader of the second generation of Lutheran reformers, stated what he saw to be the crux of the matter in his *Examination of the Council of Trent*:

> This is the issue, the point of controversy: namely, (1) what that is on account of which God receives sinful man into grace; (2) what must and can be set over against the judgment of God, that we may not be condemned according to the strict sentence of the Law; (3) what faith must apprehend and bring forward, on what it must rely when it wants to deal with God, that it may receive the remission of sins; (4) what intervenes, on account of which God is rendered appeased and propitious to the sinner who has merited eternal damnation; (5) what the conscience should set up as the thing on account of which adoption may be bestowed on us; (6) on what confidence can be safely reposed that we shall be accepted to life eternal,... whether satisfaction, obedience and merit of the Son of God, the Mediator, or the renewal which has been begun in us, the love and other virtues in us.[36]

---

36. Chemnitz, *Examination of the Council of Trent, Part I*, 468.

The Question of Justification

I agree with Chemnitz that these six points summarize well the non-negotiable elements of the gospel. If the Roman Church did indeed teach that it was our virtues, rather than the merit of Christ, that accomplished these things, it would be teaching a counterfeit gospel. However, it is in fact perfectly clear on all six points that the Roman Church teaches, as does the Lutheran Church, that these things are due to Christ's merits alone.

(1) God receives sinful man into grace on account of Christ's merits alone, since, as we have seen, the Council of Trent taught that no one can merit the initial grace of justification.

(2) and (4) It is Christ and Christ alone who has expiated our sins and propitiated God's judgment.

(3) Our sins are forgiven for Christ's sake alone: the satisfaction or penance that believers must do for grave sins after baptism do not purchase forgiveness but are subsequent to the absolution pronounced for Christ's sake.

(5) It is by the merits of Christ alone that we are adopted as sons and daughters of God and made part of God's people: "we become a member of this people not by a physical birth, but by being 'born anew,' a 'birth of water and the Spirit,' that is, by faith in Christ, and Baptism."[37]

(6) We place our confidence for eternal life in Christ and his merits: our merits have value only insofar as they connect us with Christ.

It is only on Chemnitz's sixth point that a potential difference emerges: on what can we repose our confidence that we shall be accepted to life eternal? The first five points clearly concern what Lutherans call "objective" or "universal" justification, and on this there is perfect agreement. The disagreement concerns "subjective" or "personal" justification: what within the individual Christian lays hold of this objective justification and makes it effective for him or her? Chemnitz obscures this distinction by suggesting that

---

37. Catechism of the Catholic Church, paragraph 782, p. 206.

the difference between the two Churches lies in a choice between Christ's merits and our own merits (as the basis of universal justification), rather than between faith alone and faith plus a renewed life of love (as the basis of personal justification).

The difference (faith alone versus faith completed in love) is a subtle one, since Lutherans admit that saving faith is never "alone," that is, that it is always accompanied by an inward renewal and by good works that flow from this renewed nature and that are pleasing to God. The Scriptures describe eternal life as a reward for these good works, and without good works one's perseverance in grace cannot be secure. Moreover, this inner renewal and these good works are themselves the fruit of the Spirit, the outworking of God's gracious pouring into us the death and the resurrected life of Christ. If we place our confidence that we shall be accepted to life eternal, not only upon our faith, but also upon the divine gifts of hope and love and the life that inevitably flows from these, we are still relying on Christ alone, since apart from Him we can do nothing. Here again is how the new Catholic Catechism puts it:

> The charity of Christ is the source in us of all our merits before God. Grace, by uniting us to Christ in active love, ensures the supernatural quality of our acts and consequently their merit before God and man.[38]

Is there, in the end, a significant difference between the Lutheran and Roman doctrines of justification? As we have seen, the difference is subtler than is often recognized.

- Is the difference one between a righteousness in us (*in nobis*) and a righteousness outside of us (*extra nos*), or between an inherent and an imputed righteousness? As we have seen, both sides admit that we are really made righteous by God's imputation, and both admit that this righteousness consists in a right relation to Christ.
- Does the difference consist in the issue of whether our works can be said to "merit" grace and eternal life? As we have seen,

38. Catechism of the Catholic Church, paragraph 2011, p. 487.

both sides admit that God can be said to "reward" our works with eternal life, and both admit that some of our works can be "means" of grace. This amounts to our works having a kind of "merit" (in the Roman sense).

- Does the difference concern the question of whether our works can play any causal role in securing our final glorification. As we have seen, both sides affirm Peter's injunction that we do good works to make our calling secure (2 Peter 1:10).

Insofar as there is a difference, it is grounded in the Lutherans' confusing of objective and subjective justification. Are we justified by Christ's merits alone? Yes, but who is "justified" in this sense? The whole world, believers and unbelievers alike. If we say, with the Calvinists, that Christ has died only for believers, we make faith into a human work that merits salvation in conjunction with Christ's life and passion. Roman Catholics join with Lutherans in rejecting this error: Christ's life and passion is the sole *meritorious cause* of our salvation.

If all the world is justified by Christ alone, does this mean that all will be saved? No, because not all are in a position to *benefit* from Christ's redemption. In order to be able to benefit from our objective justification, we must undergo an internal transformation that enables us to enjoy eternal life with God. Eternal life in God's presence would be no benefit to a sinful man, whose heart and mind are at enmity with God. C. S. Lewis illustrates this fact beautifully in his masterpiece *The Great Divorce*.[39] Unregenerate people would find heaven more intolerable even than hell.

How does this internal transformation take place? It *begins* with faith, which is itself a free gift of God, dependent on no prior works or merits. However, merely believing in God is not sufficient for being able to enjoy communion with God: faith must reach its natural end or completion, in the form of the love of God. Only when, through the gift of the Holy Spirit, we begin to love God are we in a state in which we can begin to enjoy the benefits of Christ's redemption. It is true, of course, that we never love as we ought,

---

39. Lewis, *The Great Divorce*.

but neither do we ever trust as we ought. The process of sanctification is a long and gradual process: the attainment of perfection is not a prerequisite of friendship with God, but the natural result of that friendship.

3

Sola Scriptura

NEXT TO THE DOCTRINE of justification, the doctrine of *sola scriptura* has played the largest role in the Roman/Lutheran controversy. The two doctrines are, of course, tightly connected. Luther was driven to the conclusion that popes, and even entire councils, can err, because his opponents were able to point out undeniable conflicts between Luther's teachings on justification and the testimony of popes, Church Fathers, and ecumenical councils.

Again, it is important to be clear about the nature of the controversy. Both sides have a very high view of Scripture: all Scripture is the very word of God, infallible in its teaching (when correctly interpreted). In addition, Rome agrees that the Scriptures are the norm of norms: all Church teaching must be interpreted so as to be consistent with the Scriptures, since Scripture and Tradition are inseparably connected.

In fact, there are really two issues here: (i) Scripture alone versus Scripture plus Tradition, and (ii) Scripture alone as the ultimate authority in theology versus Scripture as interpreted by the infallible *magisterium* of the Church as the ultimate authority. It is really the latter that is most fundamental. The issues that divide Romans and Lutherans (justification in particular) do not divide them because Rome bases its doctrines on Tradition rather than Scripture. Instead, the division comes from competing interpretations of Scripture and from the question of whether the historic episcopacy has the authority proclaim the correct interpretation. Even in the case of those doctrines on which Tradition is most relevant, such as the invocation of the saints, prayers for the dead, or the primacy of the pope, Roman theologians do not claim that these doctrines were explicitly taught by the apostles. Rather, as John Henry Newman argued in *An Essay on the Development of Doctrine*, these doctrines can be found only in an implicit and incipient form within either Scripture or Tradition. The modern-day Catholic relies, not simply on Tradition, but on the teaching authority of the Church for his or her confidence in the truth of these teachings.

It is also important to be clear about the doctrine of papal infallibility as taught by Rome. It is certainly the case that wild and extravagant claims were made for the primacy and infallibility of the pope in Luther's day. The normative doctrine of Rome is subtler and more qualified. The pope is infallible only on matters of faith and morals, and only when he speaks *ex cathedra*, that is, with the intention of speaking authoritatively on behalf of the whole Church. Similar restrictions apply to the infallibility of Church councils: their pronouncements are infallible only when they address matters of faith and morals and are intended to be authoritative statements of the teaching of the Church, and only when accepted as such by the pope. The infallible pronouncements are relatively few. Most Church councils addressed matters of practice and pastoral care, rather than doctrinal definition (Vatican II falls into this category). In modern times, papal pronouncements *ex cathedra* embrace only three doctrines: papal infallibility itself, the immaculate conception of Mary, and Mary's assumption into heaven, all of which are defensible (see sections 6 and 7).

At the same time, Lutherans do not deny altogether the authority of Church tradition. The Lutheran reaffirmation of infant baptism seems to depend, ultimately, on the fact that the Church has always practiced it, and that the practice of infant baptism has been attended with the evident bestowal of saving grace on many generations (as Luther argues in the Large Catechism). The scriptural basis for infant baptism is, as any candid Lutheran would have to admit, less than compelling. In addition, Lutherans treat the three ecumenical creeds with great respect, accepting their conclusions as matters finally closed and indisputable. Lutherans rely, somewhat uncomfortably, on their own Churchly traditions (embodied in the Book of Concord) to ensure Church unity and to provide a comprehensive guide to the interpretation of Scripture.

The central issue is not whether oral traditions from the apostles have normative status, but whether the Church has a teaching authority (*magisterium*) over the interpretation of Scripture. Or, to be more precise, whether the Church, as defined institutionally and not doctrinally, has such authority.

Lutherans can accept the idea of *magisterium*, up to a point. A layman in an orthodox congregation ought to be guided in his interpretation of Scripture by the teaching and preaching of his pastor. However, in the final analysis, it is (according to Lutherans) the responsibility of individual believers to belong to orthodox congregations and to do this they must compare the teachings of congregations and groups of congregations with the Scripture. Obviously, they cannot, without vicious circularity, rely on the teaching authority of the congregations in question to decide whether those congregations are teaching pure doctrine. For Lutherans, Scripture alone, apart from such teaching authority, must be the sole final authority for each believer.

The case for the Lutheran position

Let's look first at the case for the Lutheran position. Since both sides admit the authority of both Scripture and tradition, both sides appeal to both sources of evidence. In addition, these appeals make a good deal of sense as ad hominem arguments: if Roman Catholics can show that the Scriptures do not teach *sola scriptura* (Scripture as the sole authority), the Lutherans are hoisted by their own petard, just as Catholics would be if Lutherans could demonstrate that Tradition does teach *sola scriptura*.

A Lutheran's Case for Roman Catholicism

The Scriptures do teach the sufficiency of Scriptures for salvation and for training in righteousness (as in 2 Timothy 3:16–17), but this does not make the Lutheran case. Second Timothy 3 does not teach that the Scriptures alone are sufficient to settle all doctrinal disputes, or as the sole final authority in judging doctrine.[1] (If it did teach that, then it would entail that the Old Testament should be the only norm, since this is what Paul would have meant by "Scripture," and the New Testament canon had not yet been completed). Unfortunately for Lutherans, there are in fact no scriptural passages teaching such a doctrine. The closest we can find is Jesus' attack in Matthew 15:8–9 on the Pharisees for placing the traditions of men over the teachings of God's word. However, this isn't directly to the point, since Jesus explicitly attacks the tradition "of men," not tradition as such. Catholics will argue that they respect Divine Tradition, not the tradition of mere men. Moreover, Catholics will certainly agree that it is a sin to supplant God's Word with tradition, since any tradition in conflict with God's word is, ipso facto, not the true Tradition of the Church. In addition, there is a clear difference between pre-Christian Rabbinical traditions and post-apostolic Christian tradition: viz., Pentecost, the outpouring of the Holy Spirit, as the guide to the truth, upon the whole people of God, not merely on the prophets and judges.

The many passages that emphasize the infallibility and authority of the Scriptures as the inspired Word of God are not relevant to the dispute, since the Roman Church does not deny this. The other scriptural data cited by Lutheran theologians form quite a weak case. Paul tells the elders in Ephesus that he had taught to them the "whole counsel of God" (Acts 20:27), but this passage

---

1. As Robert Bellarmine pointed out, the phrase "all scripture" must be interpreted distributively rather than collectively: meaning "each and every scripture" rather than "scripture as a whole," since at the time of Paul's writing, the canonical Scriptures were not yet complete. Lutherans cannot use this passage to support *sola scriptura*, since it would then entail the absurdity that each and every passage of Scriptures (including, for example, some genealogy in Numbers) is by itself a sufficient norm for doctrine. We should also not overlook that this passage is immediately preceded by an affirmation of the authority of oral tradition: 2 Timothy 3:14. (*Disputations*, vol. 1, bk. IV, ch. 10.)

Sola Scriptura

makes no reference to Paul's writings, as opposed to his oral teaching. Christ often refers to Scripture as an authority in his disputes with the Pharisees (Luke 16:29; 24:27; John 5:39, 46), but he often does not.

Lutherans are quite right to point out that the authority of the Church rests on the authority of God's Word, and not vice versa. The fact that the Church is a reliable witness to the canon of Scripture does not entail that it is the Church that is responsible for making a text to be inspired by God. Obviously, it is God, rather than the Church, that is responsible for this. However, if these observations by Johannes Quendstedt or Robert Preus[2] are meant as refutations of the Roman position, they are clearly aimed at a straw man.

Evidence for *sola scriptura* from the Church Fathers is mixed, and it is in any case inconclusive. Catholics admit that Fathers can err. *Sola scriptura* is not affirmed by any creed, council, or *ex cathedra* pronouncement of a pope, and so the Roman Catholic Church cannot be charged with inconsistency on this point.

Lutherans argue that an authoritative Church is unnecessary, since the Scriptures themselves can act as the judge in any case of doctrinal controversy. This claim depends of course on the thesis of the perspicuity or clarity of the Scriptures. I have not been able to find a consistent formulation of this thesis among Lutherans. Sometimes, it is admitted that the Scriptures are not always clear (as Peter writes about some of Paul's epistles). However, if the Scriptures are not always clear, then there will be questions about which it is not clear what, if anything, the Scriptures have to say. The Lutheran position, however, depends on the claim that, on every disputed question, the Scriptures can always act effectively as the supreme court of appeal.

If we say, for example, that the Scriptures are clear only on the essential points of doctrine, we then face the problem of deciding which points of doctrine are essential and which are not. History demonstrates that Christians are as much divided on this question as they are on any question of doctrine. Lutherans have held, in

---

2 Preus, *The Inspiration of Scripture*.

fact, that every doctrine taught by Scriptures is a doctrine upon which Church fellowship hangs. The Book of Concord is an attempt (futile, in the end) to settle in advance every possible dispute about the interpretation of Scripture, in order to provide a sufficient and permanent basis for confessional unity. Many Christians believe that a far smaller set of doctrines (the Nicene Creed or, according to the Word Council of Churches, the confession that Jesus is Lord) constitutes the essential core of the gospel. One of the questions on which the Scriptures is unclear is the question of which doctrines are essential (and, by implication, the question of which doctrines are ones on which the Scriptures are clear). Lutherans must insist that the Scriptures are not only clear, but clearly clear, when they are clear, and clearly unclear, when they are unclear. Even if the Scriptures are utterly clear on all the important doctrines, unless we can all tell exactly which passages address the "important" doctrines, the Scriptures will not be able to act as the unmistakable judge in all doctrinal controversies.

However, the scriptural evidence for the absolute clarity of Scriptures is itself quite weak. Robert Preus cites passages that describe the Word of God as "nigh" to the reader (Deuteronomy 30:11–14; Romans 10:8), as well as those that describe the Word as a "light" (Proverbs 6:23; Psalm 119; 2 Peter 1:19),[3] but these fall far short of what would be required to substantiate a strong thesis of biblical perspicuity.

There is only one coherent basis for the doctrine of *sola scriptura*: an empirical, a posteriori argument that uses actual error to eliminate all other claimants to the infallible. If it can be shown that popes and councils have actually erred (by contradicting the Scriptures, for example), then the Scriptures will be left as the only remaining infallible authority. This basis places a heavy burden of proof on the Lutheran side, however. The Lutheran must demonstrate, without begging any question, that popes and valid councils (when properly interpreted) have in fact erred when proclaiming dogma (that which must be taught and believed in the Church).

---

3. Preus, *The Inspiration of Scripture*, 158.

Sola Scriptura

It is certainly true that there have been erring popes and councils. Pope Honorius I, for example, was condemned by the Sixth General Council for the error of monothelitism (the opinion that Christ had only a single faculty of willing). This is not relevant, however, since Honorius expressed some sympathy for monothelitism only as a private opinion and did not proclaim it *ex cathedra* as the doctrine of the Church. Some irregular councils, not affirmed by the pope, have proclaimed error. Other apparent errors of popes and ecumenical councils can be easily explained in similar fashion.

There is a danger of circular reasoning here. It is tempting to argue in something like the following way:

(i) *Sola scriptura* is true because popes and councils have erred.

(ii) We know that popes and councils have erred, because they have taught doctrines that cannot be supported by Scripture alone.

(iii) We know that these Church teachings are in error, because *sola scriptura* is true.

This is obviously unacceptable. To establish the truth of *sola scriptura*, Protestants must demonstrate a contradiction between a dogmatic definition of the Church and the clear and unmistakable teaching of the Scriptures on a matter of faith or morals. The demonstration of a contradiction is difficult, for two reasons. First, the matters at issue are subtle ones, and it is difficult to demonstrate that a particular interpretation of Scripture on such a subtle issue is the correct one. Second, one must also interpret Church teaching in light of the Church's explicit acceptance of the Scriptures as an infallible norm. Charity demands that the Church's teaching be interpreted in such a way as to be consistent with the Scriptures, if at all possible.

The case for the Roman Catholic position

There is evidence in Scripture for tradition: 1 Corinthians 11:2; 1 Timothy 2:2; 2 Timothy 1:13; and Jude 1:3. Jesus promises that the Holy Spirit will guide "you" (plural), that is, the whole Church, into *all* the truth (John 16:13). Paul describes the Church as "the pillar and bulwark of the truth" (1 Timothy 3:15).

As is often pointed out, the canon of Scripture was itself fixed by the teaching authority of the Church. It is surely essential that the Church recognize only canonical books (not the Quran or the Book of Mormon, for example), but this fact is inconsistent with *sola scriptura*, since the Scriptures themselves do not contain a list of which books must be included (nor even very explicit instructions about how to determine the list—is Luke or Mark an apostle?). If, as Lutherans argue, Scripture must be its own interpreter, then wouldn't it follow that the canon must be its own canonizer? And, yet, we find that this is not so, especially in the case of the New Testament canon. The New Testament gives us very little guidance about which books to treat as inspired. One might argue that Ephesians and the Revelation limit the canon to the words of "prophets and apostles," but who exactly are the apostles, in this sense, and which words count as "theirs"?

This fact results in an outright contradiction in the Lutheran position. *Sola scriptura* implies two things: that the Church must not dogmatically teach anything that is not deducible from the Scriptures (since otherwise *sola scriptura* is violated), and that the Church must dogmatically teach which books are inspired (since otherwise *sola scriptura* is empty). However, it is not possible to deduce the canon from the Scriptures. Hence, *sola scriptura* is unsustainable.

The seventeenth-century theologian Quenstedt has a clever response to this argument. He argued that we must distinguish between two senses of the canon: (1) a sense in which the canon of Scripture simply is Scripture itself, and (2) the sense of the "canon" consisting of a list or catalog of books (such as would appear as the table of contents in a printed Bible). Quenstedt insists that the first is and the second is not an article of faith.[4] Canon in the second sense is merely a matter of tradition, not binding on the believer. However, although this solution is ingenious, it is in the end unconvincing. Lutherans do in fact profess belief in the inspiration of the sixty-six books of the Protestant canon. This is not treated as an optional *adiaphora*. Indeed, it is hard to see how it could be. If an individual Christian were to embrace the canon of the ancient heretic Marcion (consisting only of a few of Paul's epistles), could the Lutheran Church really treat this as a matter of indifference, while maintaining a serious commitment to the authority of Scripture?

The Lutheran position only makes sense if we can suppose that all the doctrines can be logically deduced from the explicit statements of Scripture. That is, Lutheran theology must be completely *deductivist* in method, if it is to be coherent. In contrast, Roman theologians can legitimately make use of inductive and other "ampliative" (to use Charles S. Peirce's term) forms of inference. Roman theologians can see the doctrines of the Church emerging from the text of Scripture by a kind of organic development (as John Henry Newman argued). The Church, guided by the Holy Spirit, develops a body of doctrine that completes and fulfills God's revelatory intentions for inspired Scripture. Catholics and Lutherans can agree that Scripture is, for the most part at least, the sole foundation of all theology. (Oral tradition plays a relatively minor role in Catholic theology.) However, they differ in the forms of inference that lead from Scripture to the formulations of doctrine.

Newman makes a compelling case that the development of such doctrines as the Trinity, the two natures of Christ, and infant baptism does not fit the deductivist model. Lutheran protestations to the contrary, I cannot believe that every proposition in the Book of Concord can be deduced directly from the text of Scripture, interpreted only by means of neutral, grammatical-historical methods. At some point, one has to make judgments about which system of theology best makes sense of the biblical data, and these human judgments will be fallible and variable, except where

---

4. Quenstedt, *Theologia*, pars 1, cap. 8, sec. 5, q. 1.

superintended by the Holy Spirit. Hence the need for an infallible *magisterium* of the Church.

Some Roman Catholics claim that the Scriptures, like any text, need an authoritative interpreter. I think this claim is too broad. There are context-free meanings. These context-free meanings are sufficient to fix the central doctrines of the gospel. (Moreover, the idea that every text requires an authoritative interpreter would apply with equal force to papal and conciliar writings. Indeed, it would seem to apply to oral pronouncements as well, leading to a vicious infinite regress.) However, the context-independent meanings of the Scriptures are not in fact sufficient to settle all doctrinal disputes that must be settled (including the question of which doctrines are essential and which are not). This is confirmed by the testimony of history, including Lutheran history. If the Scriptures were perspicuous comprehensively, there would be only one major *sola scriptura* denomination, instead of hundreds.

It is hard for me to believe that God intended the Scriptures to be the sole and sufficient norm for doctrine, given their silence on so many issues that must be resolved if the Church is to function: May infants be baptized? Should those baptized by heretics or hypocrites be re-baptized? Which baptized Christians may commune, and which should not? Should repentant heretics and sinners be reconciled to the Church, and if so, how and under what conditions? Should orthodox members of schismatic sects be excommunicated? Should orthodox members of non-schismatic congregations be excommunicated, if those congregations practice improperly "open" communion? Must the threefold ministry of bishops, presbyters, and deacons be respected at all times? How are clergy (in each order) to be ordained, elected, called, or installed? Must there be at most one bishop in each city? What authority do bishops have, and what superior authority, if any, must they respect? What constitutes an authoritative council of the Church? These are matters upon which the Scriptures provide little explicit guidance, and yet, for practical reasons, it is impossible for Christians simply to agree to disagree about them.

Sola Scriptura

The *sola scriptura* position puts an impossible burden on each believer: in order to recognize true congregations, the individual believer must evaluate the congregation's confession for complete freedom from doctrinal error. To perform this task, the believer must not only believe the essential doctrines of the faith, he must know exactly which doctrines are essential and which are a matter of legitimate difference of opinion. This seems inconsistent with the variety of talents, gifts, and callings: not every believer can be expected to be a theologian. The *sola scriptura* theory condemns the majority of believers to de facto exclusion from the true Church, by virtue of their inability to distinguish truth from error on all disputed matters.

The Catholic position, in contrast, places a reasonable burden on the layman: he must simply recognize which congregations are in fellowship with that global Church that is most continuous historically with the Church of the apostles, i.e., with that Church that has the most secure claim to being the Catholic (universal) Church. In other words, the believer need master only one, relatively small set of doctrines: those concerning the identity of the true Church, not, as Lutheranism requires, an exhaustive knowledge of every disputed point of theology. This effectively limits the believer's choice to two: the Roman Catholic and the Eastern Orthodox, each of which recognizes the other as a part of the true visible Church.

To be fair, there is a kind of individual responsibility that is inescapable. The Roman Catholic layman, no less than the Protestant, must rely on his own judgment as to which Church is the visible Church in all its fullness. This burden cannot be shifted to another. However, there is a palpable and historically real difference concerning the responsibility of the individual believer under the two conceptions of the Church. For Protestants, the individual believer has only one criterion to employ: he must compare the teaching of each intercommuning set of congregations with the teaching of the Bible on every point of doctrine, or, at the very least, on every essential point. However, shifting from accuracy on all doctrinal matters to accuracy on all essential matters is, in practice, of very little help, since there is almost as much disagreement about which matters are essential as there is on the doctrines themselves. (Confessional Lutherans, for example, insist that the true Church must take the correct position, with respect to each proposed doctrine, on whether or not that doctrine is taught or implied by Scripture. Other denominations insist that a much smaller set of doctrines, perhaps just those in the Nicene Creed, form the essential core). In contrast, on the Roman Catholic view, the individual believer can recognize the true Church, not only by examining its doctrines one by one, but also by investigating its historical connection (via a physical and social chain of transmission) to the apostles. In some cases, this too can be a difficult process (for example, when there were two or even three competing "popes" during the Avignon period), but, for the most part, this has proved to be practically feasible, while the Protestant principle has utterly failed the test of history.

Here's another way of looking at the issue. The Scriptures clearly teach that the true Church will possess two essential characteristics: unity and doctrinal purity. It is only the Roman Catholic Church (and, to a degree, the Orthodox Churches) that has realized these two ends simultaneously. Conservative Protestants have maintained doctrinal purity at the price of unity, and liberal Protestants have pursued unity at the price of doctrinal consistency. Although there is certainly both doctrinal diversity and disunity within the Roman Catholic Church, it is hard to deny an impressive degree of both doctrinal consistency (at the level of official pronouncements) and institutional unity (most fundamentally, eucharistic fellowship).

The historic episcopacy

The idea of the historic episcopacy is not explicitly taught in Scriptures, although we do find all three offices (deacon, presbyter, and bishop) mentioned, and we are told that the apostles appointed presbyters in each city, and this power of appointment seems to have been itself delegated (as Paul does to Timothy and Titus).

See Acts 14:23; 20:17; Titus 1:5; 1 Timothy 3:2, 15; Hebrews 13:7, 17. However, to rule out the historic episcopacy on *sola scriptura* grounds is to beg the question. The early Fathers (Ireneaus, Cyprian, Ignatius, etc.) all teach that apostolic succession was instituted by the apostles themselves and provides a guarantee of orthodoxy.

The most fundamental question is, perhaps, that of what the Church consists in. Is there really a visible Church founded by Christ and the apostles? If so, it must have some kind of structure and hierarchy, as does every other human institution (the family, the state). This structure is not rigidly fixed: it evolves gradually over time. However, the reality of the visible Church entails that this evolving structure is there to be discovered in actual history.

On the Lutheran view, the visible Church consists of congregations, constituted by the gathering together in Christ's name of some believers (along with some hypocrites) for the sake of preaching the Word and distributing the sacraments. What this picture lacks is any sense of the visible Church as an enduring entity, constituted by the faithful transmission of truth and the successive appointment of individuals to enduring offices from one generation to the next (2 Timothy 2:2). It's as though Christ founded the Church simply by inspiring the teaching and writing of the apostles and their associates, leaving it up to each subsequent generation to re-create a visible Church *ex nihilo*, using the written record of the apostolic teaching as its only guide. One obvious problem with this picture is that the Church continued to exist after the death of the last apostles for several centuries before the canon of the New Testament was definitively recognized as such. Moreover, this picture seems to ignore the essentially historical nature of human existence, in favor of an excessively individualistic and rationalistic picture of humans as essentially disembodied and non-historical egos.

It is certainly true that God's Word is prior to and constitutive of the Church. The Church came into existence as a result of the apostles' preaching of the gospel. However, it is an error to identify God's Word with the Bible. God's Word includes the Bible, but isn't limited to it. The Church is not constituted by the Bible, since the recognition of the Bible as the permanent, normative record of God's Word was an institutional fact (the formation of the canon), which presupposed a prior institutional fact: the existence of the Church as an enduring, trans-generational society. The Church is not prior to God's Word, but it is prior to the delineation of Bible as the permanent source and standard of God's Word.

It is also impossible to define the Church as the place where the doctrines of the apostles are preserved intact. A doctrine is a teaching, and teaching is essentially articulated in the form of words. The articulation of God's Word necessarily changes as language and culture change, so it is impossible for the Church to remain absolutely static in its teaching. Inevitably, Christians face the task of distinguishing between legitimate and illegitimate expressions of the gospel in contemporary language and contemporary thought-forms, and this task cannot be accomplished through the mechanical application of grammar and logic. An element of judgment is required, and if the Church is to be maintained in its unity, there must be a final court of appeal within the Church itself and outside the text of Scripture.

When Christ promises that where two or three are gathered "in My name, there am I am in the midst of them" (Matthew 18:20), He is not implying that the mere pronouncing of the name of Jesus over an assembly is enough to constitute the Church. If it were, any congregation of Mormons, Jehovah's Witnesses, or even Muslims (who acknowledge Jesus as the Messiah) would qualify. Instead, to do something "in Christ's name" is to do it as his authorized agent, as a manager can be given the power of attorney to buy and sell in his client's name. For example, an inspired prophet speaks "in God's name" (Deuteronomy 18:19-20). Christ came in his Father's name (John 5:43). We are promised that we will receive whatever we ask in Christ's name (John 14:13, 14): not because invoking the name "Jesus" guarantees success, but because whenever we ask in accordance with God's authorization and explicit will, we can be confident of receiving what we ask for (1 John 5:14-15). Thus, to gather "in Christ's name" is to gather in the manner expressly authorized by Christ himself, under the supervision of Christ's chosen apostles, and those to whom that authority has been delegated. This does not deny God's ability to make an apostle of whomever he chooses. He appointed Paul as an apostle directly, without using any of the twelve as his instrument. However, such an appointment requires a special intervention of God and cannot be generated from below, by the human decision of an assembly of believers. This does not imply that Protestant congregations do not in any sense gather in Christ's name, but only that there are degrees of authorization, depending on the strength of a congregation's historical ties to the apostles.

Infallibility

So far, I have argued for the existence of a reliable and authoritative *magisterium*, firmly anchored in the apostolic succession of bishops headed by the pope. I have not, however, provided grounds for affirming the infallibility of the Church generally, nor of the pope specifically. There are several arguments for this further conclusion. First, there is a simple argument: the Church teaches that it is infallible; the Church is authoritative and reliable; therefore, we must believe that the Church is infallible. If the Church is infallible, and the pope is, both de facto and de jure, the head of the Church, with the power and authority to establish and enforce doctrinal standards, then the pope must be infallible in so doing (that is, when he speaks "*ex cathedra*").[5]

Here is a second, somewhat more complicated argument. Let's suppose that the Church is at least reliable and "indefectible" (to use an Anglican term) with respect to essential Christian doctrine. That is, the Church cannot err in any essential points and is very unlikely to err on any matter. We can further suppose that

---

5. The exact number of *ex cathedra* pronouncements by popes is a matter of some controversy among Roman Catholic theologians. I have seen numbers between two and twelve mentioned as possibilities. The important thing to realize is that the pope is not determined to be infallible in his private opinions or in his official actions, except insofar as he defines a dogma that must be taught by all Christians, on pain of excommunication.

the Church has these characteristics in perpetuity, since Christ's promises to the Church have no expiration date. Since theology develops over time, building on the settled conclusions reached in the past, if the Church were reliable but fallible, errors would not only accumulate over time but would actually tend to increase at a geometric or exponential rate, each error increasing the probability of further errors. Hence, a reliable but fallible Church could not remain reliable for very long. Therefore, the Church must be (at least) virtually infallible.

One final argument. If the Church were fallible but taught that it was infallible, then its erroneous belief in its own infallibility would magnify its proneness to error. A Church that wrongly believed itself to be infallible would be virtually impossible to correct. However, the Church does teach that it is infallible. Hence, it is either actually infallible or wholly unreliable. It cannot be wholly unreliable, and so must be infallible in fact.

4

Other Issues

Purgatory and praying for the dead

ON THE REMAINING ISSUES, purgatory, praying to the saints, the veneration of Mary, and the supremacy of the pope, I don't find the Catholic positions to be absolutely convincing, either on the basis of Scripture or on the basis of the traditions of the Church. However, these are relatively minor issues. None is weighty enough to justify dividing the Church. Even if we were to suppose, for the sake of argument, that the Roman Church is in error on these points, that would not justify dividing the Church.

There are, however, in each case some plausible arguments to be made for these doctrines as implicit in the Scriptures, as reasonable inferences from revelation taken as a whole.

It is certainly a serious error to place so much emphasis on purgatory that the victory of Christ over the gates of hell is minimized. Unlike hell, the saints in purgatory are fully assured of their salvation and filled with joy and peace. The fact that the purgatorial state might involve some laborious and even painful toil should not obscure the fact that is the entrance hall to heaven. To its credit, the Catholic Church has moved a long way from the overemphasis on purgatory that characterized the period of the

Reformation. In the new Catholic Catechism, for example, the discussion of purgatory takes up only four pages.

It is noteworthy that God does not instantaneously transform believers into a state of sinlessness at the moment of conversion. Instead, God invites us to cooperate in a gradual process of sanctification. This seems to follow from God's respect for the integrity of the development of our personalities. He transforms us by persuasion and assistance, not coercively or violently. Given these facts, it is reasonable that our transition to sinlessness after death (the healing of our sinful proclivities) will also be a gradual one, requiring our willing cooperation. That such a continued process of sanctification might involve, as it does in this life, a measure of loving discipline also seems probable.

If any of this is even possibly true, it is reasonable to pray for believers who have died. Why should death be a barrier to our love and concern, given that Christ, through his life, death, and resurrection, has utterly defeated it?

The Lutheran confessions claim that purgatory is inconsistent with the doctrine of salvation by grace alone, since the latter doctrine dispels doubt, while the doctrine of purgatory creates doubt (Melanchthon's *Apology*, the Smalcald Articles).[1] This seems an exceedingly weak argument. The doctrine of purgatory does not create doubt about one's final state: souls in purgatory are irreversibly bound for heaven. It doesn't create any doubt about the love or favor of God: the trials of purgatory are acts of loving discipline, not the expression of divine wrath or retribution.

Praying to the saints

It is hard to see how asking the saints in heaven to pray for us is any more problematic than asking fellow believers on earth to do so. The Epistle of James teaches us that the intercession of a righteous man accomplishes much (James 5:16).

---

1. Melanchthon, *Apology of the Augsburg Confession*, article XII (Book of Concord, 80); Luther, Smalcald Articles, Part III, articles II and III (Book of Concord, 138, 144).

The only reasonable barrier to this is doubt about whether the saints in heaven can hear our requests for prayer. Their awareness of our struggles would seem to be an implication of the communion of saints, as professed in the Apostles' Creed.

The standard Lutheran objection, found already in the Augsburg Confession, is an argument from scriptural silence: the Scriptures do not command us to pray to the saints, in heaven, they nowhere provide an example of such prayer, and they offer no assurance that the saints are able to hear our prayers.

There are a few scriptural passages that suggest that the saints in heaven might well be aware of us. In the book of Revelation 8:3–4, the saints of heaven are praying before God's throne, and in Revelation 6:10 the martyred saints are aware that their blood has not yet been avenged. In Hebrews 12:1, we are described as surrounded by a "cloud of witnesses," which would seem to include angels and departed saints. If they are witnesses of our lives, they are certainly able to pray for us in specific terms and respond to requests for prayer.

In any case, arguments from silence are quite weak. There are many things that Christians do simply because doing so makes sense. The Scriptures nowhere command us to conduct wedding ceremonies or funerals in our churches, but Christians have always done so (with the exception of a few fundamentalist sects that rely on exactly the same sort of argument of silence used by Lutherans against the invocation of the saints). We are told that the prayers of a righteous man accomplish much (James), and we know that Christ has defeated death. How could Christ's victory over death be complete if death represents an unbreachable chasm between believers on earth and those in heaven?

Mary

The veneration of Mary is a hedge around the doctrine of the incarnation. If Jesus is truly God, then Mary is truly the Mother of God. His uniqueness implies her uniqueness. To treat Mary as simply an ordinary woman puts at risk either the deity or the true humanity of Christ.

Mary is described in Luke 1:28 as "highly favored." The Roman Catholic Church has interpreted this as meaning that Mary is the full realization of the vocation to sainthood that is shared by all believers. She is the paradigmatic member of the Church: she is fully now what the Church as a whole is destined to be. Just as we are all destined to "judge the angels," she is appropriately described as the queen of angels and of heaven.

The immaculate conception of Mary, God's supernatural protection of her from the effects of original sin, seems a reasonable inference in light of the uniquely intimate relation between her and Jesus. Would it really be appropriate for the incarnate Son of God to be borne and reared by a woman in the grip of original sin?[2]

Mary's sinlessness throughout her life is consistent with her need for a Savior. Like us, she is saved by grace alone, for Christ's sake (as Pope Pius IX explicitly stated when defining the dogma). The only difference is that God placed her in this state of grace from the moment of her conception and maintained her in it throughout her life, as is appropriate, given her unique vocation.

Some Roman theologians and devotional practices describe Mary as a co-mediator (or mediatrix, the feminine version of the noun) with Christ (this has not been made a dogma and so is not an opinion to which all Catholics must subscribe). This would be blasphemous if it were understood as giving Mary a mediatorship parallel to and of the same order as Christ's (as, indeed, the unfortunate prefix "co-" seems to suggest). However, all Roman theologians are quick to insist that Mary's mediating role is rather comparable to that held by all believers, who are a royal priesthood (1 Peter 2:9) and ambassadors of Christ (2 Corinthians 5:20).

---

2. Throughout his life, Luther maintained, as a private opinion, a very nearly Roman position on Mariology, a fact not often mentioned in Lutheran Churches today. For example, Luther apparently believed to the end in Mary's perpetual virginity, her immaculate conception, and the Christian's duty to venerate her. See *Luther's Works*, vol. 4, 694; vol. 51, 128–29.

Similarly, when Mary is described as a *co-redemptrix*, this in no way implies that there is any kind of equality or parallelism between Christ's role as redeemer and Mary's. Mary played a unique role in God's plan of redemption through Christ by allowing herself to become the mother of Christ (Luke 1:28), performing a paradigmatic act of obedience in contrast to Eve's paradigmatic disobedience. However, it is Christ's life, death, and resurrection that have redeemed us: Mary's obedience served merely as a subordinate instrument.

It is true that there is a real conflict between Roman Mariology and the extreme form of monergism espoused by Luther and Calvin. Mary's role as co-redemptrix highlights the fact that Christians are not utterly passive in the process of salvation, i.e., that we genuinely cooperate with God's grace. This synergism is compatible with the fact that, in the final analysis, our salvation is God's work alone, since even our acts of cooperation are the results of his grace. The Lutheran rejection of any positive human role is incompatible with sound Christology, since it is essential to our redemption that Christ be true man as well as true God. Humanity is not utterly passive in our redemption by God, since Christ, the God-Man, is the redeemer.

Some Lutherans and Protestants have argued that Marian devotion results from the intrusion of paganism (the cults of Isis, Astarte, or Diana) into the Church. First of all, this claim is in some conflict with the argument that Marian devotion is a late, medieval development. There's no evidence of the survival of the worship of Isis or Diana in twelfth-century Europe. Second, the same sort of claim could be made about all of Christian theology. There are many pagan precursors of a dying and rising god, for example. I find plausible the hypothesis proposed by C. S. Lewis and J. R. R. Tolkien that pagan mythology is itself a kind of preparation for the gospel, a distorted foreshadowing of the true myth of the gospel. If so, it may be that the pagan worship of the virgin goddess or Earth Mother was a kind of crude anticipation of Mary's role as Mother of God and Mother of the Church.

There are some Marian practices that seem excessive to me. Some language used in Marian devotion has to be understood as, at best, poetic hyperbole. However, such excessive devotion is not required by Rome, and any idolatrous interpretations of these words and practices are explicitly disavowed. For example, if any Catholic thinks of Mary as a merciful go-between, whose intercessions are needed to soften the severity of Christ the judge, this is a gross error and no part of the Catholic faith. Mary's mercy is derived from Christ's greater mercy: she is merciful as an imitator and disciple of Christ.

The Mass as a sacrifice

Roman Catholic theology describes the Mass, the celebration of the Eucharist, as a propitiatory sacrifice, the "unbloody" offering by a human priest of Christ's body and blood. This account was emphatically reaffirmed at the Council of Trent, despite very persuasive arguments on the part of many Roman theologians that such an account was in flagrant contradiction to Hebrews 7:27, which states that Christ offered up a sacrifice for sins "once for all when He offered up Himself," and Hebrews 9:12, "through His own blood He entered the holy place once for all."

This presents another stark choice between a charitable and uncharitable construction. Interpreted uncharitably, the teaching of Trent seems to deny the uniqueness and sufficiency of Christ's sacrifice on the cross, and the uniqueness of his high priesthood. However, more recent theology, as expressed in the new Catechism of the Catholic Church, offers an acceptable interpretation: there is only one Sacrifice (on the cross) and only one Priest (Christ himself). The Mass consists simply of that one sacrifice offered by that one priest, made sacramentally present.[3] The human priest's actions are Christ's own actions, just as it is God who baptizes and God who offers absolution through the agency of his human ministers. If we affirm, as Lutherans must, the real presence of the

---

3. Catechism of the Catholic Church, paragraphs 1356–67, pp. 342–44.

Christ's body and blood in the sacrament, then we cannot deny that Christ's one sacrifice of that body and blood is also really present.

There remain two important differences between the Lutheran and Roman Catholic theories of the Eucharist. First, on the Roman view, the performance of the Mass can benefit even those who do not partake of the elements: spectators, and those for whom the benefit of the Mass is intended. In the past, private masses, in which only the celebrating priest communed, were common, but these have been, since Vatican II, actively discouraged as incompatible with the inner logic of the sacrament. This is connected with the fact that, according to Rome, Christ offers his body and blood in the Mass not only to the communicants, but also to the Father (but again, not as a separate offering from the one on the cross, but merely through making present again that one sacrifice). Second, Roman Catholic theology understands the benefit of the Mass to include, not only communion as a means of grace, but also the satisfaction of the temporal penalties for sin and the accumulation of "merit." That is, it counts participation in (directly or indirectly) the Mass as a good work. This seems a reasonable position, given the rest of Catholic doctrine.

The primacy of the pope

Admittedly, the scriptural arguments for Peter's supremacy are inconclusive, at best. James seems to have presided over the first Church council, and Paul is adamant in insisting that his own authority derives directly from his calling by God and does not depend on Peter's acknowledgment of it.

The best argument for it is that Christ clearly intended that the Church should be visibly one, empirically united in love (especially Christ's extended prayer in John 17, highlighting verse 21). Since God willed the end, he must also have willed a sufficient means. History clearly teaches that such visible unity is impossible without a single office to which all good-faith doctrinal and ecclesiastical disputes can be referred. Christ promises that the Spirit will guide the Church (collectively) to the truth (John 16:13).

Thus, in my view, recognizing a duty to submit to the authority of the pope does not depend on believing that there was a direct, permanent divine appointment of the pope as Christ's vicar or representative on earth. The visible Church must be a single, unitary institution of some kind, and such a unitary institution must have an enduring structure of authority. Within a given location, this authority would require a supervisor or bishop. The global unity of the Church requires an office that recognizes, on behalf of the whole Church, which individual is in fact the bishop of each jurisdiction. Historically, this role has been played by the five patriarchs (Jerusalem, Antioch, Alexandria, Constantinople, and Rome), with the patriarch of Rome as first among equals. This picture certainly grants an authority to the pope less grandiose than was claimed by many in Luther's time. There is no basis for any temporal authority of the pope, and the worldwide recognition of the freedom of conscience is a great boon to the Church. However, it remains the case that the Church is in need of a visible focus of unity, and only the papacy is capable of fulfilling that role.

Does the pope rule the Church by a divine right or merely a human one? The answer lies somewhere in between. The papacy did not receive a direct, once-and-for-all grant of a specific form of authority. The authority of the pope depends on the facts of history, and it could change as circumstances change. Pope John Paul II, for example, indicated that the role of the papacy might be altered as a means of achieving reconciliation between the Roman Catholic Church and the Eastern Orthodox. This would make no sense if the authority of the papacy was fixed and unalterable.[4]

In addition, I would not claim that the pope's role as the successor of Peter can be found stated, even implicitly, in the text of the New Testament. At the same time, with the hindsight of two

---

4. What I have said in this section falls short of the official teaching of Rome, but my point is that a strong case for Roman Catholicism can be made without assuming a strong doctrine of a fixed and permanent form of papal authority. The text should be taken as reflecting my thought at a particular, transitional moment.

millennia, it is difficult to believe that the prominence of Peter in the Gospels as the spokesman of the apostles, the involvement of Peter and Paul in the establishment of the congregation in Rome and their martyrdom there, and the subsequent importance of the office of the bishop of Rome are mere coincidences. The references to Peter's confession as a foundational rock for the Church (Matthew 16:18) and Jesus' charge to Peter to care for his flock (John 21) should be seen as figures and prophecies of the crucial role that Peter's successors were to play (as John Henry Newman argued in *An Essay on the Development of Christian Doctrine*[5]).

As Newman argues, the recognition of the central authority of the pope developed gradually over time. The same logic that led the Church to acknowledge the monarchical authority of each bishop in his diocese (namely, the need for local unity and order), drove the Church to find the role of the pope as "center of unity" and supreme judge within the community of bishops to be indispensable in practice. Looking backward from the vantage point of this historical experience, it is easy to find many statements and events that are indicative of papal supremacy. As Newman argued, it is necessary "to interpret the words and deeds of the earlier Church by the determinate teaching of the latter."[6]

Could the success of the Eastern Orthodox Church over the last 1,000 years (since the great schism in 1056) in maintaining both unity and orthodoxy be proof that the papacy is not in fact needed? Although this is undoubtedly an impressive feat, there are some reasons for thinking that it does not in fact establish the possibility of unity without central authority. Throughout most of the past one thousand years, the unity and theological consistency has in fact been imposed upon it by a central authority: the Byzantine empire for the first 400 years, and the Russian Tsar for much of the remainder. This arrangement has sometimes been called, perhaps unfairly, one of "caesaropapism" (i.e., a situation in which Caesar plays a papal role). Secondly, during nearly all of the period when the caesaro-papist situation failed, the Eastern Church found

5. Newman, *Development of Doctrine*, 145ff.
6. Newman, *Development of Doctrine*, 145.

itself under both severe persecution (under Islam or Soviet Communism) and state regulation. For example, under the Ottoman Empire, the emperor delegated broad powers over the Christian community (including the Church) to the ecumenical patriarch of Constantinople. A similar arrangement was imposed by the Communists upon the Russian Orthodox Church. The only difference between the pope, on the one side, and the Byzantine emperor or patriarch of Constantinople, on the other, is that only the former can plausibly be denominated the "successor of Peter," and that only the former was recognized by the early Church as first in honor among all bishops. There is nothing in Scripture or the early acts of the Church that would suggest that the Roman emperor or the ecumenical patriarch in Constantinople was destined for any special responsibility for the unity of the Church.

The acid test for papal necessity is the experience of Eastern Orthodox Churches in North America, and here the results are not encouraging. In the United States, the Orthodox Churches enjoy liberty without state regulation, exactly the sort of condition most liable to division and doctrinal confusion. In America, the fifteen independent, ethnically defined (autocephalous) Churches of the East have been unable to achieve anything like a normal, episcopal structure. It is axiomatic for Catholics and Orthodox alike that there should be a single ruling bishop in each metropolitan area. The Orthodox bishops in America are divided along ethnic lines, with massively overlapping jurisdiction. There are no signs of progress toward regularity, thanks to the decline in the power and authority of the patriarch of Constantinople, and the virtual insignificance of the apostolic sees in Antioch, Jerusalem, and Alexandria.

Conclusion

I HAVE NOTHING BUT great affection and feelings of gratitude toward the Lutheran Church. The Holy Spirit used that Church to give and nurture a saving faith in Christ to generations of my forebears, to myself, and to my children. The Word was preached there and the sacraments dispensed, and the fruits of the Spirit have been very much in evidence in the lives of dedicated service and zeal. Many elements of the Catholic tradition have been faithfully preserved for generations among Lutherans, including a high view of the Scripture and the sacraments, an appreciation for the value of the creeds and the teachings of the Church Fathers, and an acknowledgement of the historical survival and continuity of the Church from the time of the apostles until today. Insofar as there were errors in Lutheran teaching, they were errors largely motivated by holy desire to rely on Christ alone and to honor Christ alone.

There are, however, grave dangers in cutting oneself off from the Roman Catholic Church. In particular, the guidance of the Holy Spirit is promised to the Church as a whole, not to each individual or to isolated sects. As time passes, Protestant and Lutheran church bodies experience a powerful temptation to conform their teachings to the spirit of the times, to the assumptions and cultural worldviews of their own nations and generations. The Roman Church has the great advantage of spanning both time and place in a nearly comprehensive fashion. Moreover, Christ himself commands us to seek and maintain unity.

Epilogue

I WAS IN 2007 one of history's slowest and most reluctant converts to Catholicism. I entered the Church not out of any dissatisfaction with Lutheranism or out of any special attraction to the spirituality, aesthetics, or sanctity of Catholics. My decision was driven purely by an intellectual conviction that the Reformation was founded upon a number of theological errors. I felt that my commitment to Christ and to the Church demanded that I bring my life into conformity with my theological discoveries.

Frankly, I expected my life as a Catholic to be little different from my life as a sincere and fervent Protestant. In fact, I feared that much would be lost on a practical and aesthetic level. I loved, and still love, the traditional hymns and liturgical music of the Lutheran tradition, and I worried that I would find few Catholics with an interest in the study of the Bible, and many (perhaps an overwhelming majority) whose faith and practice were lukewarm at best. I'm happy to report that all of this pessimism has proved utterly unfounded.

The one great thing I didn't anticipate is what a profound difference the reception of the full range of Catholic sacraments would have on my spiritual development. The sacrament of penance and reconciliation and, of course, that of the Eucharist have freed me from many self-destructive vices that I had come to think of as inevitable features of human life, and I have seen a renewal of spiritual growth and development in my fifties and sixties that I would have thought impossible for someone so fixed in habits and character. I've also enjoyed a richness of fellowship in the Church with people from many different lands and backgrounds. I entered the forbidding gates with great fear and trembling, but I've found my true home on the other side.

APPENDIX A

Commentary on the Council of Trent

Session V

Canons

5. If anyone denies that by the grace of our Lord Jesus Christ which is conferred in baptism, the guilt of original sin is remitted, or says that the whole of that which belongs to the essence of sin is not taken away, but says that it is only canceled or not imputed, let him be anathema. For in those who are born again God hates nothing, because there is no condemnation to those who are truly buried together with Christ by baptism unto death, [Romans 6:4] who walk not according to the flesh, [Rom. 8:1] but, putting off the old man and putting on the new one who is created according to God [Ephesians 4:22, 24; Colossians 3:9f], are made innocent, immaculate, pure, guiltless and beloved of God, heirs indeed of God, joint heirs with Christ [Romans 8:17]; so that there is nothing whatever to hinder their entrance into heaven. But this holy council perceives and confesses that in the one baptized there remains concupiscence or an inclination to sin, which, since it is left for us to wrestle with, cannot injure those who do not acquiesce but resist manfully by the grace of Jesus Christ; indeed, he who shall have striven lawfully shall be crowned [2 Timothy 2:5]. This

concupiscence, which the Apostle sometimes calls sin [Romans 6–8; Colossians 3], the holy council declares the Catholic Church has never understood to be called sin in the sense that it is truly and properly sin in those born again, but in the sense that it is of sin and inclines to sin. But if anyone is of the contrary opinion, let him be anathema.

This canon clearly contradicts the authoritative Lutheran position. The issue is this: at baptism, is sin merely not imputed to the believer (Lutheran) or is it actually taken away (Roman)? Is what remains (concupiscence, the tendency to sin) actually hateful to God, but simply not hated for Christ's sake (Lutheran), or is it, in and of itself, inoffensive (Roman Catholic)? This is no mere verbal dispute over the word *sin*. The canon admits that there is a permissible use of the word *sin* to refer to mere concupiscence: a use modeled by Paul himself in Romans and Colossians. The Lutherans are not being condemned merely for calling concupiscence "sin" but for teaching that the reconciled believer remains a sinner in the sense that his internal condition elicits God's wrath and condemnation, which wrath and condemnation must be perpetually canceled and annulled by reference to the extrinsic merits of Christ.

I don't want to overstate the difference, however. The Roman Church admits that *all* believers (even the most saintly) sin daily (Session VI, Chapter XI; 1 John 1:9), and that these venial sins are not obstacles to God's grace or to the believer's persistence and growth in grace. However, these venial sins are products of our weakness and immaturity and do not so alienate us from God as to make the continuance in God's grace and favor impossible. These venial sins are forgiven for Christ's sake, but this forgiveness is not merely *forensic* in nature. Our baptismal grace is also a perpetual source of healing and renewal, in such a way that these venial sins leave no enduring mark on the believer that would bring him under the hatred or enmity of God (although they may have temporal consequences or incur temporal "punishment," in the form of loving, fatherly discipline).

The passages cited by the canon (from Romans 6 and 8, and from Ephesians and Colossians) do not rule out the Lutheran position. The absence of condemnation mentioned in Romans 8 is explicitly a forensic notion. The real question is simply this: can God fail to impute (forensically) sin that remains (ontologically) in the believer; or, equivalently, can sin remain ontologically in one to whom God has imputed a state of innocence (sinlessness)? There are two reasons to doubt that it can: (1) The absence of condemnation affirmed in Romans 8 follows the analogy of dying, being buried, and being raised with Christ in Romans 6. Baptism effects death and resurrection, which surely refers to an internal change. (2) Since God is omnipotent, his word is always effective. Hence, a declaration of sinlessness by God must immediately effect a real state of sinlessness in the believer. This internal state is not a mere consequence or by-product of the divine declaration, but is an essential part of it, without which the divine action would be incomplete.

The concupiscence that remains in the believer is not the basis for continuing divine wrath, but rather for divine forbearance and mercy ("the spirit is willing but the flesh is weak").

Session VI

Decree on Justification

Chapter I. On the Inability of Nature and of the Law to justify man.

> ... they were so far the servants of sin, and under the power of the devil and of death, that not the Gentiles only by the force of nature, but not even the Jews by the very letter itself of the law of Moses, were able to be liberated, or to arise, therefrom; although free will, attenuated as it was in its powers, and bent down, was by no means extinguished in them.

APPENDIX A

This chapter reflects the Roman Catholic interpretation of Romans 1–4. The inability of persons to be justified by "works of the law" is taken to include both efforts by Gentiles to conform to the law of nature and efforts by Jews to keep the law of Moses (including the moral, as well as the ceremonial and civil law). This inability is not extended to those fruits of the Spirit that result from God's love being poured into our hearts (Romans 5:5) as a result of the gift of the Spirit and our baptism into Christ's death and resurrection (Romans 6). Through the new life of the Spirit, initiated by faith in Christ, we are enabled to fulfill the law.

This chapter is also directed against the theory, propounded in Luther's *The Bondage of the Will* and in the Heidelberg Disputation, that freedom of the will was utterly lost in the fall.[1] Luther's view was never incorporated into the normative confessions of the Lutheran Church. In fact, Luther's monergism[2] was implicitly rejected by the synergism (or semi-synergism) of the Formula of Concord,[3] in which it is insisted that human beings who do not

---

1 "However, with regard to God, and in all that bears on salvation or damnation, he has no 'free-will,' but is a captive, prisoner and bondslave, either to the will of God, or to the will of Satan." Luther, *On the Bondage of the Will*, 107.

2. "But why the Majesty does not remove or change this fault of will in every man (for it is not in the power of man to do it), or why He lays this fault to the charge of the will, when man cannot avoid it, it is not lawful to ask; and though you should ask much, you would never find out; as Paul says in Rom. 11: 'Who art thou that repliest against God?' (Rom. 9:20)." Luther, *On the Bondage of the Will*, 170. See also 340.

3. Lutherans deny that their position is aptly described as "synergistic," but the Formula of Concord clearly teaches a position that could be called "negative synergism": we cooperate in our reception of grace simply by not effectually resisting it, as we are all free to do:

> All those who obstinately and persistently resist the operations and movement of the Holy Ghost, which take place through the Word, do not receive, but grieve and lose, the Holy Ghost. (Thorough Declaration, II Of Free Will, Book of Concord, 249.)

> The cause of this contempt for the Word is not God's foreknowledge [or predestination], but the perverse will of men, which rejects or perverts the means and instruments of the Holy Ghost, which God offers him through the call, and resists the Holy Ghost, who wishes to be efficacious, and works through the Word, as Christ says (Matt. 23:37). (Thorough Declaration, XI Of God's Eternal Election, Book

come to faith do so because they choose to resist the Holy Spirit. In *The Bondage of the Will,* Luther insisted that all believers are converted despite the fact that they, no less than any unbeliever, whole-heartedly resisted the Holy Spirit prior to conversion. Like Calvin, Luther attributed the distinction between the elect and the non-elect to the inscrutable, "hidden" will of God. Trent and the Formula of Concord are essentially in agreement and in opposition to both Luther and Calvin: although no one can repent and believe without God's assistance, our free will remains substantial enough to be able to choose between effectively resisting God's grace and not doing so.

Chapter II. On the dispensation and mystery of Christ's advent.

> ... that all men might receive the adoption of sons, Him God hath proposed as a propitiator, through faith in his blood, for our sins, and not for our sins only, but also for those of the whole world.

This is in full agreement with the Lutheran position: that Christ alone propitiates for our sins, and that the atonement is universal in scope.

Chapter III. Who are justified through Christ.

> But, though He died for all, yet do not all receive the benefit of His death, but those only unto whom the merit of His passion is communicated.... If they were not born again in Christ, they never would be justified; seeing

---

of Concord, 290.)

But the reason why not all who hear it believe, and some are therefore condemned the more deeply, is not because God has begrudged them their salvation; but it is their own fault, as they have heard the Word in such a manner as not to learn, but only to despise, blaspheme and disgrace it, and have resisted the Holy Spirit, who through the Word wished to work in them. (Book of Concord, 293.)

... the damned, who themselves, and not God, have prepared themselves as vessels of damnation. (Book of Concord, 293.)

> that, in that new birth, there is bestowed upon them, through the merit of His passion, the grace whereby they are made just.

Lutherans and Roman Catholics agree in rejecting universalism. The benefits of Christ's passion must be communicated to each through the new birth (John 3). Even the last phrase should be acceptable to Lutherans: the righteousness we receive through faith is a real righteousness, not a mere fiction. We are actually made just or righteous by God's declaration.

Chapter V. On the necessity, in adults, of preparation for Justification, and whence it proceeds.

> The beginning of the said Justification is to be derived from the prevenient grace of God, through Jesus Christ, that is to say, from His vocation, whereby, without any merits existing on their own, they are called; that so they, who by sins were alienated from God, may be disposed through His quickening and assisting grace, to convert themselves to their own justification, by freely assenting to and co-operating with that said grace . . . yet he is not able, by his own free will, without the grace of God, to move himself unto justice in His sight.

On this point, Lutherans, Reformed Christians, and Roman Catholics are in agreement, in opposition to Pelagians of all kinds. God's grace is not received only after conversion but is active before and during conversion. As Luther puts it in the Small Catechism, we are not able, of our wisdom or strength, to repent or believe in Christ. These are worked in us by the Holy Spirit.

At the same time, Lutherans can concede that we are not passive in the manner of a stone or other inanimate object. Energized and assisted by God's grace, our wills are active in the process of repenting and turning to Christ.

Chapter VI. The manner of preparation.

> Now they (adults) are disposed unto the said justice, when, excited and assisted by divine grace, conceiving faith by hearing, they are freely moved towards God, believing those things to be true which God has revealed and promised,—and this especially, that God justifies the impious by His grace, through the redemption that is in Christ Jesus; and when, understanding themselves to be sinners, they, by turning themselves, from the fear of divine justice whereby they are profitably agitated, to consider the mercy of God, are raised unto hope, confiding that God will be propitious to them for Christ's sake; and they begin to love Him as the fountain of all justice ...

This chapter again makes clear that faith and repentance are the work of the Holy Spirit, using God's word as the means. It also rejects any Pelagian or semi-Pelagian supposition (of the kind espoused by nominalists like Ockham and Biel) that our efforts, merits, or righteousness in any way precede the grace of God. Nor will Lutherans deny that the justified begin to love God truly.

Chapter VII. What the Justification of the impious is, and what are the causes thereof.

> This disposition, or preparation, is followed by Justification itself, which is not remission of sins merely, but also the sanctification and renewal of the inward man, through the voluntary reception of the grace, and of the gifts, whereby man of unjust becomes just, and of an enemy a friend, that so he may be an heir according to hope of life everlasting.

Lutherans will object to the use of the term *justification* to include what Lutherans would call *sanctification*. It is true that the Greek word for "justification," and its cognates, are judicial or forensic in character. Lutherans will insist that sanctification and renewal are effects of justification and do not belong to its very essence.

APPENDIX A

Nonetheless, they will admit that they are necessary and inseparable effects.

What is the basis of the Lutheran distinction between justification and sanctification? As I explained above, the forensic character of the verb "to justify" does not force a real distinction between justifying and sanctifying. When a forensic declaration is issued by an omnipotent God, the declaring is a real making, and so legitimately described as the act of sanctifying the believer. In fact, the Scriptures, and even Paul himself, often use the word *sanctify* in contexts that imply its equivalence to *justify*: 1 Corinthians 6:11; 2 Thessalonians 2:13; Acts 26:18; 1 Corinthians 1:2; John 17:17, 19; Hebrews 10:10; 13:12; 1 Peter 1:2. See also the use of "renewal" or "regeneration" in Titus 3:4–7. The word *justify* may be forensic, but *sanctify* (to make holy) is surely transformational in meaning.

> ... the efficient cause is a merciful God who washes and sanctifies gratuitously . . . the meritorious cause is His most beloved only-begotten, our Lord Jesus Christ . . . merited Justification for us by His most holy Passion . . . and made satisfaction for us unto God the Father . . . we are not only reputed, but are truly called, and are, just, receiving justice within us, each one according to his own measure, which the Holy Ghost distributes to every one as He wills . . . The said justification of the impious, when by the merit of that same most holy Passion, the charity of God is poured forth, by the Holy Spirit, in the hearts of those that are justified, and is inherent therein: whence, man, through Jesus Christ, in whom he is ingrafted, receives, in the said justification, together with the remission of sins, all these gifts infused at once, faith, hope and charity. For faith, unless hope and charity be added thereto, neither unites man perfectly with Christ, nor makes him a living member of His body.

This is, as Christopher Malloy has recently argued, the heart of the Council's decree.[4] It makes use of Aristotle's well-known fourfold distinction of "causes" or "explanations": efficient, final,

---

4. Malloy, *Engrafted into Christ*.

material, and formal, with the addition of a fifth, meritorious. Christ's passion is listed as the sole meritorious cause of the redemption of humankind. This means that Christ and Christ alone has earned for us the right to forgiveness, reconciliation, and the adoption as sons and daughters of God. There is no room left here for other human merits to supplant or supplement the unique place of Christ.

For our purposes, the crucial claim is that there is, within the believer, a formal cause of righteousness that is ontologically distinct from both the primeval righteousness of God and the attained righteousness of Christ. The formal cause of something is that actuality by which the thing exists and is the kind of thing it most fundamentally is. Thus, Trent is teaching that the righteousness of the believer is something internal to him: a kind of disposition or arrangement of the soul. This internal disposition consists in the supernatural virtues of faith, hope, and love that are poured into the believer's heart by the Holy Spirit. It is not faith alone, but faith, hope, and love that together unite the believer to Christ, constituting him as a righteous person, rightly related to God.

From a Lutheran perspective, this teaching takes back everything that the thesis that Christ's passion is the meritorious cause of our righteousness promised to secure for us. The Tridentine formulation threatens to make the connection between Christ's work and my own righteousness a remote and merely historical one: without Christ's passions, the means of grace would not now be offered to me, but given what Christ accomplished long ago, my present justification has nothing directly to do with him, but only with my own diligence in seeking to make the most of the gifts that are now offered.

However, none of this distancing of Christ's work from the believer's righteousness is explicitly stated in the chapter. The relationship between the two can be as close and as intimate as one could hope (as the metaphor of "engrafting" suggests), so long as it falls short of being identity in the strict sense. My righteousness cannot be simply identical to Christ's righteousness, if the real distinction between Christ and myself is to be maintained and a collapse into pantheism avoided. This chapter implies that my righteousness consists in being united with Christ, which suggests that my internal state wouldn't constitute righteousness apart from that union. Although my righteousness is internal, it is not wholly intrinsic to me: it is not a state that would please God and bring me into communion with him apart from the work and person of Christ.

If we are to take seriously the idea of *solo Christo* (by Christ alone), that all men are forgiven and reconciled to take only for Christ's sake, and not at all for reason of any internal condition, then we are led inevitably to the thesis of universal or general justification. God imputes Christ's righteousness to all men, believers and non-believers alike, since otherwise we would have to think of our faith as a kind of merit that is added to Christ's. However, this general justification is not of benefit to all persons, but only to believers in Christ. Why is this? It must be because faith is a precondition to our being able to enjoy the beatific vision, eternal life in God's presence. But why is faith a prerequisite for this? Roman Catholic theologians have a logical answer: because only those who love God can enjoy his presence, and it is only through faith in Christ that we are led to participate in the sacramental life of the Church through which this love of God is poured into our hearts by the Spirit. As the book of Hebrews explains, we cannot please God without faith, since we must believe that God exists and is the rewarder of those who seek him (Hebrews 11:6).

Whatever condition it is that distinguishes the saved from the unsaved, this condition must be (at least in part) an internal one, since all people are included in general justification, and God is no respecter of persons. According to Lutherans, this internal condition consists entirely of faith (although saving faith is incompatible with mortal sin). Why, on the Lutheran view, is faith needed? One might try to answer this, as do some Arminians and American Evangelicals, in terms of God's respect for human free will: faith is merely our consent to receiving the offered gift of salvation, and God will not force that gift on the non-consenting. This answer is barred to Lutherans, and for good reason, since it amounts to a kind of semi-Pelagianism. It conceives of faith (in the form of such consent) as a human work, independent of God's grace. In fact, God's free gift of salvation includes the conversion of the unwilling and non-consenting into the willing and consenting. Why, then, is faith and faith alone required? Regeneration and inner renewal are also the free gifts and work of God—why must these be excluded from the required internal condition?

Without the love of God infused into our hearts, we are in no condition to enjoy the blessings of eternal life. Eternity in the presence of a God whom we hate and fear is no blessing. The forensic declaration of righteousness can benefit us only by the reception of an internal condition that itself constitutes a form of righteousness: one wholly dependent at every moment on Christ's righteousness, yet metaphysically distinct, just as we are in Christ and yet distinct from him.

It is important to recognize that the formal "cause" is not the *cause* of our justification in the modern sense of the word, one that corresponds to the Aristotelian efficient (or, perhaps the efficient and meritorious) cause. The efficient cause is God, who justifies gratuitously. We do not *cause ourselves* to be just or *make ourselves* just through any inner quality or habit or external action. God, and God alone, is the efficient cause of our transformation through his grace.

Chapter VIII. In what manner it is to be understood, that the impious is justified by faith, and gratuitously.

> And whereas the Apostle saith, that man is justified by faith and freely, those words are to be understood in that sense which the perpetual consent of the Catholic Church hath held and expressed; to wit, that we are therefore said to be justified by faith, because faith is the beginning of human salvation, the foundation and the root of all Justification; without which it is impossible to please God, and to come unto the fellowship of His sons; but we are therefore said to be justified freely, because that none of

> those things which precede justification—whether faith or works—merit the grace itself of justification.

Here Trent unambiguously rejects the opinion of some scholastic philosophers (including Scotus and Ockham) that it is possible to merit justification by any merely human action. The grace of justification is given freely, apart from any prior merit. Thus, Pelagianism and semi-Pelagianism are clearly excluded, and the Pauline teaching of grace as a free gift, received apart from works, is clearly affirmed. We are justified by faith because faith alone is the beginning, foundation, and root of all justification: faith is the critical juncture through which all of God's grace is communicated to the benefit of the justified.

Chapter IX. Against the vain confidence of Heretics.

> For even so no pious person ought to doubt of the mercy of God, of the merit of Christ, and of the virtue and efficacy of the sacraments, even so each one, when he regards himself, and his own weakness and indisposition, may have fear and apprehension touching his own grace; seeing that no one can know with a certainty of faith, which cannot be subject to error, that he has obtained the grace of God.

This chapter excludes only an infallible knowledge of one's own salvation, comparable to the certainty that one has in the articles of faith themselves. It does not rule out a very real certainty and assurance of salvation; it simply means that my own salvation should not be included among the affirmations of a creedal sort. As the chapter emphasizes, there are good reasons for a faithful Christian to feel confidence before God: the mercy of God, the merit of Christ, and the efficacy of the sacraments. What the chapter recommends is that the believer focus attention outward, on the promises and character of God, as the object of faith, and not turn inward on a fruitless enterprise of verifying with certainty that his or her own faith is genuine.

An element of uncertainty of this kind is inevitable in any theological system that does not affirm universal salvation. If salvation is not universal, then there is some condition that distinguishes the saved from the others, and there is no way, apart from some special divine revelation, that the individual Christian could achieve infallible certainty that he satisfies this condition, whether the condition is faith alone or faith formed in love. Thus, if I believe in justification through faith alone, and I want to achieve an absolute assurance of my salvation, I face the insuperable obstacle of verifying the genuineness of my faith (trust and confidence) in Christ.

Chapter X. On the increase of Justification received.

> ... they, through the observance of the commandments of God and of the Church, faith co-operating with good works, increase in that justice which they have received through the grace of Christ, and are still further justified, as it is written, He that is just, let him be justified still.

This chapter brings out a second crucial difference between the Roman Catholic and Lutheran theories of justification. On the Lutheran view, there is no room for an increase in justification, since the justification of the Christian consists simply in his receiving the imputation of Christ's perfect righteousness. This imputation is a matter of all or nothing: either I have a saving faith in Christ, or I do not. Sanctification is a matter of degree, but sanctification and justification are utterly distinct.

There is some tension within the Lutheran position concerning the sacraments (especially the Eucharist) as means of grace. Communion is supposed to provide the believer with both forgiveness of sins and an "increase" of faith. If faith can be increased, then it would seem to follow that justification itself is a matter of degree: the more faith one has, the more of Christ's righteousness one is able to appropriate. Alternatively, one could think of the "increase" of one's faith as consisting in its becoming more robust and enduring, increasing the likelihood of one's persevering in faith until death. On this view, a linkage between justification and sanctification is created, since the increase of one's faith is a matter of sanctification, and one's final salvation depends upon one's persevering in faith until the end. Thus, faithful use of the means of grace is a way of making one's calling and election sure (2 Peter 1:10).

Lutherans insist that all human actions be excluded from the means of grace. The preaching of the Word is the action of God speaking through the human preacher. It is God who baptizes, using the human agent as a mere instrument (baptizing in the name of the Trinity). It is God who proclaims forgiveness through the absolution uttered by the human minister. Lutherans consistently exclude actions of the believer himself from the category of means of grace, including prayer, worship, and acts of charity. However, this Lutheran position seems confused. When a believer prays, it is the Holy Spirit himself who prays through us, as Paul teaches in Romans 8. In fact, everything the believer does in faith is in fact the action of Christ: Galatians 2:20. Thus, there is no reason why prayer, worship, and acts of charity cannot be means of grace, as many scriptural passages seem to suggest.

Chapter XI. On keeping the Commandments, and on the necessity and possibility thereof.

> For, although, during this mortal life, men, how holy and just soever, at times fall into at least light and daily sins, which are also called venial, not therefore do they cease to be just. For that cry of the just, Forgive us our trespasses, is both humble and true.

If one sought to be justified by the law, apart from grace, one would have to keep the law perfectly, as Paul teaches. However, those who are enlivened by the Holy Spirit can fulfill the law, despite daily falling into sin. How is this possible? For two reasons: first, the fruit of the Spirit have an infinite value, that overwhelms the flaws resulting from our sin-prone natures (what Paul calls "the flesh" or "the old Adam"). Second, because the grace poured into our hearts by the Holy Spirit provides for an ongoing healing and remission of sins, so long as the sin is venial, rather than mortal.

Lutherans agree that those who commit mortal sins do not continue in a state of grace but must be reconverted and restored. A mortal sin involves a deliberate rejecting of God's grace, cutting the fallen Christian off from the source of forgiveness and renewal.

Chapter XIV. On the fallen, and their restoration.

> ... the penitence of a Christian, after his fall, is very different from that at his baptism; and therein are included not only a cessation from sins, and a detestation thereof, or, a contrite and humble heart, but also the sacramental confession of the said sins,—at least in desire, and to be made in its season,—and sacerdotal absolution; and likewise satisfaction by fasts, alms, prayers, and other pious exercises of a spiritual life; not indeed for the eternal punishment, which is, together with the guilt, remitted, but for the temporal punishment, which, as the sacred writings teach, is not wholly remitted...

This chapter introduces two crucial issues: the need for sacramental confession and absolution after the commission of mortal sin, and the reality of "temporal punishment" for sin. Although Lutherans retain the practice of confession and absolution (including, at least in theory, private confession before an ordained minister), they deny that such absolution is necessary for restoration, even in the form of a sincere desire for such absolution. Lutherans see absolution (the so-called "Office of the Keys") as a valuable aid to the restoration of the fallen, but not as essential. Instead, the fallen should simply look back to his or her own baptism as the sufficient channel of grace that is always available, when appropriated by faith.

This is an issue that is difficult to adjudicate on the basis of Scripture alone. However, Christ's institution of the Office of the

Keys seems to imply a sacerdotal role for the apostles and their successors, over and beyond merely proclaiming the forgiveness of sins through the preaching of the gospel. Lutherans admit that recourse to sacramental absolution is greatly to be encouraged and commended. If such sacramental assurance of forgiveness is available, and the penitent obstinately refuses to make use of it, this indicates disrespect for, and even damnable contempt for, God's offer of pardon.

On the matter of "temporal punishment," there is ample scriptural basis for the idea that God, as a matter of fatherly discipline, allows us to suffer negative consequences as a result of our sin. The example of David's loss of his son in the aftermath of the adultery with Bathsheba (2 Samuel 12) is an excellent example of this. David had repented and was no longer under the wrath or judgment of God, yet God allowed the child to die as a way of disciplining David. The use of acts of devotion and charity as an expression of our sorrow and as tokens of respect for God in the aftermath of serious sins seems fully appropriate.

It is important to recognize that, in the Roman Catholic practice of penance, the absolution offered to the penitent is unconditional and absolute. The subsequent acts of "satisfaction" do not earn the forgiveness of sins: forgiveness and renewal is freely offered by God's grace through the sacrament. Acts of satisfaction are further means of increasing in grace and in friendship with God.

Chapter XV. That, by every mortal sin, grace is lost, but not faith.

> The received grace of Justification is lost, not only by infidelity [unbelief] whereby even faith itself is lost, but also by another other mortal sin whatever, thought faith not be lost . . .

Lutherans teach that mortal sins are merely reliable indicators that saving faith has been lost. It is impossible for one possessing saving faith to commit such sins. Trent teaches that mortal sins deprive the sinner of the grace of justification, even if faith itself is not lost. In this case, the difference appears to be merely verbal. Trent uses the word *faith* in a narrow sense, to refer to assent to the revelation of God (what Lutherans call "historical knowledge"). Saving faith, for Lutherans, includes an act of trust in Christ. Roman Catholic theologians are not bound to say that it is possible for someone who genuinely trusts in Christ to commit a mortal sin.

Chapter XVI. On the fruit of Justification, that is, on the merit of good works, and on the nature of that merit.

> Life eternal is to be proposed to those working well unto the end, and hoping in God, both as a grace mercifully promised to the sons of God through Jesus Christ, and as a reward which is according to the promise of God Himself, to be faithfully rendered to their good works and merits. For this is that crown of justice which the Apostle declared was, after his fight and course, laid up for him, to be rendered to him by the just judge, and not only to him, but also to all that love his coming ... Thus, neither is our own justice established as our own as from ourselves; nor is the justice of God ignored or repudiated: for that justice which is called ours, because that we are justified from its being inherent in us, that same is (the justice) of God, because that it is infused into us of God, through the merit of Christ ... Nevertheless, God forbid that a Christian should either trust or glory in himself, and not in the Lord, whose bounty towards all men is so great, that He will have the things which are His own gifts be their merits.

Three important points are covered here: (1) eternal life can be correctly described as a "reward" for our good works and merits, (2) our righteousness is really infused in us by God, through the merits of Christ, and (3) we must not trust or glory in ourselves or our works but only in God and his gifts. On the point of reward, Trent's position is well supported by the Scriptures. Even

Melanchthon admits this in the *Apology*.[5] To say that God rewards our works with eternal life is not to say that we earn eternal life (in the sense placing God in our debt), or that our works have merit apart from their source in the righteousness of Christ, or that the merit of these works is comprehensible either to the worker himself or to other human observers. Our works are rewarded by eternal life according to God's gracious promise. The works themselves are the gifts of God, the fruit of the Holy Spirit in our lives. They merit eternal life by establishing our union and identification with Christ, not by virtue of their intrinsic, natural qualities. This is why we cannot trust or glory in ourselves or in our works. Instead, we must always look exclusively to God and his grace: we must trust that, for Christ's sake and in accordance with his promises, he will work in us those things needed as prerequisites for receiving eternal life. The just are not even conscious of having performed these works, as Jesus teaches. We do nothing autonomously, of ourselves, as Christ teaches in the parable of the vine (John 15).

Canons

Canon 1. If anyone says that man can be justified before God by his own works, whether done by his own natural powers or through the teaching of the law, [chapters I and III] without divine grace through Jesus Christ, let him be anathema.

Canon 2. If anyone says that divine grace through Christ Jesus is given for this only, that man may be able more

---

5. "Just as the inheritance and all possessions of a father are given to the son, as a rich compensation and reward for his obedience, and yet the son receives the inheritance, not on account of his merit, but because the father, for the reason that he is his father, wants him to have it. Therefore, it is a sufficient reason why eternal life is called a reward, because thereby the tribulations we suffer, and the works of love which we do, are compensated, although we have not deserved it. For there are two kinds of compensation: one, which we are obliged, the other, which we are not obliged, to render." (Melanchthon, *Apology to the Augsburg Confession*, Article III, 66–67.)

> easily to live justly and to merit eternal life, as if by free will without grace he is able to do both, though with hardship and difficulty, let him be anathema.
>
> Canon 3. If anyone says that without the predisposing inspiration of the Holy Ghost [chapter V] and without His help, man can believe, hope, love or be repentant as he ought, [Romans 5:5] so that the grace of justification may be bestowed upon him, let him be anathema.

These first three canons clearly and unambiguously reject any form of Pelagianism or semi-Pelagianism. We can do nothing of ourselves, apart from God's grace. Even repentance and faith are the work of God's Spirit within us. Christ's grace does not simply make it easier for us to do what, in principle, we could have done on our own. Apart from Christ, we were utterly unable to make ourselves fit for eternal life.

> Canon 4. If anyone says that man's free will moved and aroused by God, by assenting to God's call and action, in no way cooperates toward disposing and preparing itself to obtain the grace of justification, that it cannot refuse its assent if it wishes, but that, as something inanimate, it does nothing whatever and is merely passive, let him be anathema.

Canon 4 rejects the thesis, shared by Luther and Calvin but later renounced by the Formula of Concord, that saving grace is irresistible. Although awkwardly worded, the canon does not mean to suggest that the free will can perform some sort of "preparation" of itself prior to God's grace, since this "preparation" is clearly stated to be the result of being "moved and aroused by God."

> Canon 5. If anyone says that after the sin of Adam man's free will was lost and destroyed, or that it is a thing only in name, indeed a name without a reality, a fiction introduced into the Church by Satan, let him be anathema.

Canon 5 is clearly aimed at Luther's *The Bondage of the Will*, in which human beings are described as donkeys ridden either by

APPENDIX A

God or the devil, with no choice between the two.[6] By excluding free will utterly, Luther is forced to a doctrine of double predestination, according to which the fate of the damned is due to the inscrutable, "hidden" will of God. This position was later repudiated by the Lutheran Church.

> Canon 6. If anyone says that it is not in man's power to make his ways evil, but that the works that are evil as well as those that are good God produces, not permissively only but also *propria et per se*, so that the treason of Judas is no less His own proper work than the vocation of St. Paul, let him be anathema.

This again is directed against *The Bondage of the Will*, in which Luther discusses the case of Judas.[7] According to Luther, the sin and subsequent damnation of Judas are due to the inexorable plan of God, foreknown from all eternity.

> Canon 7. If anyone says that all works done before justification, in whatever manner they may be done, are truly sins, or merit the hatred of God; that the more earnestly one strives to dispose himself for grace, the more grievously he sins, let him be anathema.

Canon 7 is directed against some early statements by Luther: for example, in the *Heidelberg Disputation against Scholastic Philosophy*.[8] This canon does not contradict canons 1 through 3: it does not teach that works done before justification can in any way merit justification or eternal life. Nor does it imply that it is, even

---

6. "So, man's will is like a beast standing between two riders. If God rides it, it wills and goes where God wills: as the Psalm says, 'I am become as a beast before thee, and I am ever with thee' (Psalm 72:22–23). If Satan rides, it wills and goes where Satan wills. Nor may it choose to which rider it will run, or which it will seek; but the riders themselves fight to decide who shall have and hold it." Luther, *On the Bondage of the Will*, 103–4.

7. Luther, *On the Bondage of the Will*, 206, 220–22.

8. Consider, for example, theses 9 and 10:
   9. To say that works without Christ are dead, but not mortal, appears to constitute a perilous surrender of the fear of God.

   10. Indeed, it is very difficult to see how a work can be dead and at the same time not a harmful and mortal sin.

in principle, possible for the unregenerate to avoid all damnable sins. However, the canon denies that all works of non-believers are sinful and deserving of God's enmity. Luther argued that every work performed apart from Christ, no matter how noble in human terms, is a violation of the First Commandment, implicitly rejecting the way of righteousness prescribed by God (namely, faith in Christ). This strikes me as overreaching on Luther's part. It is true that, for Christians, "whatever is not of faith is sin" (Romans 14:23), but this does not obviously apply to non-believers, who are acting without, and not against, faith. Non-believers are capable of acting in accordance with the natural law, and God judges such actions justly. If all actions apart from Christ were equally mortal sins, there would be no room for degrees of judgment in hell, which the Scriptures clearly teach.

> Canon 8. If anyone says that the fear of hell, [Matthew 10:28; Luke 12:5] whereby, by grieving for sins, we flee to the mercy of God or abstain from sinning, is a sin or makes sinners worse, let him be anathema.

I'm not sure who this canon is aimed at, but it certainly says nothing that a Lutheran should object to. The fear of hell is worked in us by the preaching of the law, a necessary prerequisite to our justification through the gospel.

> Canon 9. If anyone says that the sinner is justified by faith alone [chapters VII, VIII], meaning that nothing else is required to cooperate in order to obtain the grace of justification, and that it is not in any way necessary that he be prepared and disposed by the action of his own will, let him be anathema.

This canon, along with canon 10, are the crux of the matter. Trent teaches that faith is the beginning, root, and foundation of justification, but faith alone is not sufficient as a channel through which one is united with Christ and by which one receives the benefit of his merits. Faith must attain its natural end (as is described in 1 Peter 1), a state in which faith is combined with hope and love. As far as hope is concerned, it would seem that the dispute is merely verbal: Trent limits the meaning of "faith" to intellectual assent to God's revelation, while Lutherans include within saving faith the element of trust and confidence in Christ that corresponds closely to the Roman Catholic conception of hope. However, on the question of the role of the love of God poured into us by the Holy Spirit, there would seem to be a real difference. It is here that the Lutheran Reformers depart sharply from Augustine's view of justification, which identified justification with the believer's coming to love God for his own sake through the infusion of God's grace. Lutherans insist that the love of God is the natural consequence of justification, but not in any sense a requirement or prerequisite of it.

The main Lutheran objection (found clearly in Melanchthon's *Apology*) to the inclusion of love as a means of justification is the danger it poses to the assurance of salvation, since, as Melanchthon puts it, we never love God as we ought. True enough, although it is equally true that we never trust God as we ought. Trent does not teach that the quality of our love of God must reach a certain level before we can count as justified: in particular, it never teaches that we must love God perfectly, as the saints in heaven do. However, were faith and hope utterly devoid of love, how could a person be in a state of friendship with God, prepared for eternal life in God's presence? Trent is not teaching that we must love God in order to earn our salvation, or in order to put God in our debt, but merely that the presence of God's love in our heart, through the agency of God's grace, is as much a condition of our being reconciled to God as is the presence of faith and hope. As Paul puts it, what matters is "faith working in love" (Galatians 5:6).

In the second clause of the canon, the Tridentine fathers reiterate the importance of our voluntary cooperation with God's grace. This cooperation is itself made possible by God's prevenient grace, but the individual human being is not passive in the way that an inanimate object would be, but the will must cooperate with God's grace in the formation of faith, hope, and love. Without this element of synergism, the monstrosity of double predestination cannot be avoided, as Luther's *The Bondage of the Will* demonstrates.

> Canon 10. If anyone says that men are justified without the justice of Christ, [Galatians 2:16; supra, chapter VII] whereby He merited for us, or by that justice are formally just, let him be anathema.

The first clause is a clear affirmation of *solo Christo*: it is only by the righteousness of Christ that we are justified. In the second clause, it is again affirmed that there is a created form of righteousness that is brought about within the believer by God's Spirit, a form that is ontologically distinct from Christ's own righteousness. If this were not so, then the sanctification of the believer would result in his annihilation and the reduplication within his body of Christ's human soul. The connection between our righteousness and Christ's is an exceedingly intimate one: the relation of participation. However, to be righteous by participation in or union with Christ is not to have the numerically the very same individual form of righteousness that informs Christ's own soul. Rather, the relation is like that of the life of the branch and that of the vine (John 14).

> Canon 11. If anyone says that men are justified either by the sole imputation of the justice of Christ or by the sole remission of sins, to the exclusion of the grace and the charity which is poured forth in their hearts by the Holy Ghost [Romans 5:5] and remains in them, or also that the grace by which we are justified is only the good will of God, let him be anathema.

Although this canon is often cited as a stumbling block to a common confession between Lutherans and Roman Catholics, in fact it says nothing that a Lutheran need deny. Read carefully, it does not deny that justification consists in imputation of righteousness and remission of sins, but it merely requires that this imputation not be thought of in a way that excludes regeneration and renewal by the Holy Spirit. Lutherans do not deny the existence of a necessary connection between justification and regeneration, and so they do not teach that we are justified by imputation "to the exclusion of" the indwelling of the Holy Spirit and his gifts.

> Canon 12. If anyone says that justifying faith is nothing else than confidence in divine mercy [chapter IX], which remits sins for Christ's sake, or that it is this confidence alone that justifies us, let him be anathema.

This canon doesn't in fact condemn the Lutheran position, since Lutherans admit that saving faith involves more than confidence in divine mercy: it also includes an element of intellectual assent to the articles of faith, as well as a sorrow and hatred toward one's own sins, as a result of the convicting power of God's law. Here, the Tridentine fathers seem to have misunderstood the Lutheran position to be one in which the confidence that one's sins have been forgiven is somehow self-validating. However, Lutherans need not deny that it is possible for sinners to have what the Formula of Concord describes as a false and "Epicurean" confidence in one's salvation. Those who persist unrepentantly in mortal sin must not be deluded into thinking that they remain in a state of grace.

> Canon 13. If anyone says that in order to obtain the remission of sins it is necessary for every man to believe with certainty and without any hesitation arising from his own weakness and indisposition that his sins are forgiven him, let him be anathema.

There's nothing in the Lutheran position that requires that one's faith be believed with certainty and without hesitation. It is the object of faith, and not its quality, that justifies. However, this canon does allude to a serious difficulty for Lutheran theology. Lutherans want to insist both that, one the one hand, the sacraments do not convey forgiveness and reconciliation to the sinner apart from true faith, and, on the other hand, that the believer should seek the assurance of his salvation by looking outward, to God's promise, and not inward, to his own faith. This outward-looking assurance, which Lutherans prize, is better secured by the Roman doctrine that the sacraments work *ex opere operata*, without any precondition within the recipient, so long as the recipient interposes no positive obstacle (in the form of deliberate hypocrisy). When the Lutheran hears his pastor say, "Your sins are forgiven," he must (if he is to take into account the whole of Lutheran doctrine) add a proviso: "if I truly believe." Thus, the assurance of forgiveness is conditional on his introspective knowledge of his own belief, rather than being dependent only on his knowledge of God's faithfulness.

> Canon 14. If anyone says that man is absolved from his sins and justified because he firmly believes that he is absolved and justified, [chapter IX] or that no one is truly justified except him who believes himself justified, and that by this faith alone absolution and justification are effected, let him be anathema.

This canon simply repeats the points made in the preceding two.

> Canon 15. If anyone says that a man who is born again and justified is bound ex fide to believe that he is certainly in the number of the predestined [chapter XII], let him be anathema.

> Canon 16. If anyone says that he will for certain, with an absolute and infallible certainty, have that great gift of perseverance even to the end, unless he shall have learned this by a special revelation [chapter XIII], let him be anathema.

Canons 15 and 16 clearly aimed at an error outside the camp of orthodox Lutherans. It is impossible for one to know with certainty that one is numbered among the elect, since this depends on whether one will endure in saving faith until death, and there are no infallible, advance indicators of this fact.

> Canon 17. If anyone says that the grace of justification is shared by those only who are predestined to life, but that all others who are called are called indeed but receive not grace, as if they are by divine power predestined to evil, let him be anathema.

APPENDIX A

This condemnation of double predestination is apt, with respect to Luther's *On the Bondage of the Will*, but it does not pertain to the normative Lutheran position, as enunciated in the Formula of Concord.

> Canon 18. If anyone says that the commandments of God are, even for one that is justified and constituted in grace [chapter XI], impossible to observe, let him be anathema.

Lutherans should also agree with this canon, since justification brings with it regeneration and renewal through the gift of the Holy Spirit, which enables believers to fulfill the moral law and perform works pleasing to God.

Thus, of all the anathemas concerning original sin and justification, there are only three that are relevant to the normative Lutheran position of the Book of Concord: the fifth canon of Session V, and the ninth and tenth canons of Session VI. Two of these canons (V, 5 and VI, 10) reject the Lutheran thesis that justification consists in the believer's acquiring an external (*extra nos*), "alien" righteousness: the very righteousness of Christ imputed to the believer. However, Lutherans do not deny that an inner transformation of regeneration and renewal always necessarily accompanies justification; they simply deny that this regeneration is to be included within the act of justification. Lutherans insist that our being acceptable to God involves no reference to this internal transformation, which is merely a by-product or proper accident of justification. However, this Lutheran doctrine of the alien righteousness of Christ seems to confuse objective and subjective justification. The righteousness of Christ is the meritorious cause of the redemption of all of humankind: it is the sole basis on which all persons, believers and unbelievers alike, are made acceptable to God. The alien righteousness of Christ is imputed to all of mankind. However, this imputation is of benefit to an individual human being only when that human being has been so transformed as to be capable of enjoying eternal friendship with God. This transformation begins with faith (the beginning, root, and foundation of justification), but it must culminate in the love of God being poured into our hearts.

For this reason, canon 9 of Session VI is correct in denying that faith alone is sufficient to unite the believer to Christ. This issue is complicated somewhat by the fact that the Tridentine fathers limit "faith" to intellectual assent, while Lutherans use "saving faith" to include an active trusting in Christ as one's Savior (similar to the Roman Catholic conception of "hope"). The real issue concerns the role of love or charity. For Lutherans, the love of God and of neighbor is a necessary consequence of an individual's being made right with God, but one's standing in a state of grace is in no way dependent on this internal disposition. Roman Catholics see faith, hope, and love as all three essential to one's continuing to stand in the state of grace.

Lutherans concede that it is possible to lose one's salvation. All who commit mortal sins have sundered themselves from Christ and are in need of reconversion. Lutherans also concede that we can help to make our calling and election sure through the diligent practice of good works (2 Peter 1:10).[9] Growth in grace and the avoidance of mortal sin depend on our love for God; hence, love is essential to our remaining in a state of grace. Moreover, the Scriptures clearly teach that eternal life is a reward for love and for the works of love: Galatians 5:6; Romans 2:6-8; 2 Timothy 4:8; James 2:24; Revelation 22:12. This love is not a human work: it is a gift of God's grace, for Christ's sake: Romans 5:5; 8:4; 1 Corinthians 6:10; Galatians 2:20-22; 5:18; 6:15; 2 Thessalonians 2:13; Acts 26:18; Hebrews 10:14; 1 Peter 1:2.

If the Tridentine position on justification involves a damnable reliance on human effort and human merit, then the same is true of St. Augustine himself. If the Council of Trent is semi-Pelagian, so was Augustine. This is the *reductio ad absurdum* of the Lutheran position. Calling Augustine a *Pelagian* is like calling Abraham Lincoln a copperhead, Churchill an appeaser, or Abraham an anti-Semite. Augustine clearly taught that we are saved by grace alone

---

9. Melanchthon's *Apology*, Article XX (Book of Concord, 104), and Formula of Concord, Thorough Declaration IV (Book of Concord, 258).

through Christ alone, but an individual is a beneficiary of this grace only when the capacity for the true love of God is infused in his heart through union with Christ. Faith alone is sufficient to initiate this process, but the process must continue throughout life through the increase of faith, hope, and love brought about by a growth in grace. This growth in grace, in turn, is made possible through our cooperation in good works of all kinds, not simply by our passively receiving the repeated promise of forgiveness.

APPENDIX B

Commentary on Lutheran and Roman Catholic Proof Texts concerning Justification by Faith

I. Lutheran Proof Texts[1]

A. Pauline Epistles

Romans 3:21-26

21But now a righteousness from God, *apart from law,* has been made known, to which the Law and the Prophets testify. 22This righteousness from God comes through faith in Jesus Christ to all who believe. There is no difference, 23for all have sinned and fall short of the glory of God, 24and are justified *freely by his grace* through the redemption that came by Christ Jesus. 25God presented him as a sacrifice of atonement, through faith in his blood. He did this to demonstrate his justice, because in his forbearance he had left the sins committed beforehand unpunished—26he did it to demonstrate his justice

---

1. Quotations from the Bible in this appendix are from a popular translation created by Evangelical scholars, The New International Version (Colorado Springs, CO: International Bible Society, 1984). I used the NIV so that I could not be accused of choosing a translation biased toward Catholicism.

at the present time, so as to be just and the one who justifies those who have faith in Jesus.

Some Roman Catholic apologists, following St. Jerome, argue that Paul's use of "the law" in this passage refers merely to the ceremonial aspects of the Mosaic law, such as circumcision, that have been superseded by the New Covenant. This seems implausible, especially since Paul uses, in chapter 7, the prohibition of coveting (clearly a permanent, moral aspect of the Law of Sinai) as his example of a typical prohibition.

In any case, the Council of Trent takes Paul to be referring here both to the natural moral law, inscribed in the hearts of Gentiles, and to the Law of Sinai, available only to the Jews. Neither law provides the means for salvation, since fallen human nature prevents us from acting in a way acceptable to God. The damage of original sin is too profound to be reversed by any autonomous human effort. God's grace, available only through faith in Christ, is absolutely necessary.

This passage is silent on whether this righteousness, which comes to us from God through faith in Christ, is internal or external, inherent or "alien." It is silent, further, on the question of whether this righteousness is received *in toto*, all at once, or whether the believer can be expected to grow from one degree of righteousness to another. Nor does the passage speak to the question of whether such growth (if it is required) depends only on the believer's faith, or whether the believer cooperates in that growth through subsequent actions. Even if the believer uses the law to guide him in this cooperation with God's Spirit, this would not nullify the fact that God's righteousness came to him initially apart from the law. What Paul is condemning is the use of the law by the autonomous, self-righteous sinner as a means for manipulating or controlling God, placing God under an obligation to accept as he is, without receiving Christ's righteousness through faith.

According to Paul, we are justified freely by God's grace, implying that there is nothing that we can do, prior to our conversion to faith, that could be thought of as earning that grace or mitigating the guilt of our sinfulness. In this sense, righteousness comes to us "apart from law": no conformity to the law is a prerequisite to the initial reception of God's grace.

Paul makes it clear that faith is the first point of contact between the sinner and God's grace: it is to the believer in Christ that the righteousness of God is freely given. Trent describes faith as the "beginning, root and foundation of all justification." However, Paul does not explicitly teach that faith alone suffices for the continued growth and maturation of that righteousness, to the exclusion of hope and love.

Romans 4:2–5

> 2If, in fact, Abraham was justified by works, he had something to boast about—but not before God. 3What does the Scripture say? "Abraham believed God, and it was credited to him as righteousness."

> 4Now when a man works, his wages are not credited to him as a gift, but as an obligation. 5However, to the man who *does not work but trusts* God who justifies the wicked, his faith is credited as righteousness.

This is a critically important passage, often cited by Lutherans and Protestants in support of a purely forensic conception of righteousness. The word for "credits" is *logizomai*, a word that means to think or to estimate, especially to ascribe value to. Very much the same meaning attaches to the Hebrew word *chashab*, which occurs in the Genesis passage (Genesis 15) that Paul is quoting, following the Septuagint translation. The words *logizomai* and *chashab* do not carry any connotation of mere supposition or make-believe: in most cases, they express the holding of an accurate belief and estimation. Consequently, when God, who is omniscient and omnipotent, reckons something, that reckoning is true and just. God reckons Abraham's faith to be righteousness; he appraises the value of Abraham's faith as constituting righteousness.

The passage does not directly support Melanchthon's theory of imputation: it does not say that God reckons Christ's (extrinsic, alien) righteousness to be Abraham's righteousness. Rather, it says that God reckons Abraham's *faith* to be Abraham's righteousness. Why is this? Why is Abraham's faith of such value? Here all Christians will agree: because Abraham's faith lays hold of Christ. But, how does it do that? Faith lays hold of Christ by uniting us to Christ through baptism (Romans 6), and by keeping us united to Christ through the gift of the Spirit (Romans 8). There is certainly nothing in this passage to indicate that our union and conjunction with Christ is a purely external matter. Hence, it does not support the Lutheran conception of the alien righteousness of Christ, as opposed to the Roman Catholic doctrine of an internal appropriation of Christ through the infusion of grace and the Spirit.

Moreover, Paul typically uses the words for "work" and "to work" (variants of *ergon*) with a negative connotation, signifying things done autonomously, apart from Christ. The one exception is Romans 2:6, where Paul is quoting the Septuagint and uses *ergon*, or "deed," in a neutral sense. (Ephesians 2:10, if this letter is in fact Pauline, is a second exception.) Throughout his letters, Paul rarely uses *ergon* to refer to the fruit of the Spirit or the results of walking or living in the Spirit. In Ephesians 2:20, the one exception to this rule, Paul combines the word *work* with the qualifier "good" and with the phrase 'to walk in them' (*peripateo*), a phrase with a consistently positive connotation for Paul. Hence, there is little reason to take him to be here excluding the fruit of the Spirit from any role in justification. In the context of Romans 4, it is likely that "work" is shorthand for "work of the law of Sinai," since Paul's point is that faith in Christ equalizes Jews and Gentiles, limiting the significance of the law of Moses.

Romans 4:6–9

6David says the same thing when he speaks of the blessedness of the man to whom God credits righteousness *apart from works*:

> 7 "Blessed are they
>   whose transgressions are forgiven,
>   whose sins are covered.
> 8 Blessed is the man
>   whose sin the Lord will never count against him."
> 9 Is this blessedness only for the circumcised, or also for the uncircumcised? We have been saying that Abraham's faith was credited to him as righteousness.

We see in this passage the same characteristics: the pejorative use of the word *work* (*ergon*), the use of "credit" (*logizomai*), implying a truthful estimation of the believer's righteousness and sinlessness. All this is consistent with a transformational conception of justification, with faith as the channel through which transforming grace is conveyed. God does not "count" our sins because he has, by his grace, annihilated them.

The root of the word for "forgive" (*aphiemi*) gives the sense of *sending away*. What God forgives, he removes. The fact that sin is described as "covered" does give some support to a fictional or suppositional form of righteousness, if we think of the sin as a blemish that is hidden or disguised by the covering. However, we could instead think of the covering as a fulfilling a real need: supplying raiment to the naked sinner or bandages to his wounds. Similarly, the saints in heaven are described as having robes washed white by the blood of the Lamb. This cannot be taken as suggesting that even the saints in heaven remain internally sinful, with a mere covering to disguise this fact. The covering with a clean robe signifies a corresponding, internal cleanliness. (This is not to deny that the metaphor indicates that there is a forensic element in justification, in additional to the transformational one.)

Romans 4:16

> 16 Therefore, the promise comes by faith, so that it may be by grace and may be guaranteed to all Abraham's offspring—not only to those who are of the law but also to

those who are of the faith of Abraham. He is the father of us all.

The context of this verse makes clear that "the law" refers specifically to the Torah, the Law of Moses. For Paul, there is clearly an essential connection between grace and faith. Salvation must be out of (*ek*) faith if it is to be according to (*kata*) grace. The key contrast here is between the faith of Abraham and observance of the Law of Moses. By giving priority to the first, Paul secures the equality between Gentile and Jewish Christians, since both have access through faith in Christ to God's saving grace. This does not establish that grace conveys a merely external righteousness or legal status, nor does it exclude the possibility of the Christian believer's active cooperation with God's grace, outside of the Law of Moses.

Romans 5:1-2

1Therefore, since we have been justified through faith, we have peace with God through our Lord Jesus Christ, 2through whom we have gained access by faith into this grace in which we now stand. And we rejoice in the hope of the glory of God.

Faith provides access or introduction (*prosagage*) to God's grace, and those who stand in that grace are at peace with God. This is consistent with the necessity of cooperating actively with God's Spirit in order to continue within grace and grow in grace.

Romans 5:17

17For if, by the trespass of the one man, death reigned through that one man, how much more will those who receive God's abundant provision of grace and of the gift of righteousness reign in life through the one man, Jesus Christ.

Commentary on Proof Texts

Just as Adam's sin condemned his descendants by bequeathing to them a corrupted internal nature, so too are those who receive the gift of Christ's righteousness transformed within. The provision of grace and the gift of righteousness are identical to a new life in Christ.

Romans 10:9

> 9That if you confess with your mouth, "Jesus is Lord," and believe in your heart that God raised him from the dead, you will be saved. 10For it is with your heart that you believe and are justified, and it is with your mouth that you confess and are saved.

The verbal confession that Paul refers to is probably that associated with the sacrament of baptism. He is referring to the role that faith plays in introducing us to a state of grace. He is not guaranteeing that a single act of belief and confession is sufficient to guarantee one's eternal destiny, since it is certainly possible to fall from grace.

1 Corinthians 1:30-31

> 30It is because of him that you are in Christ Jesus, who has become for us wisdom from God—that is, our righteousness, holiness and redemption. 31Therefore, as it is written: "Let him who boasts boast in the Lord."

In saying that Christ has "become" our righteousness, Paul cannot mean that Christ himself is the formal cause of each believer's righteousness (that internal disposition by which the believer is righteous), since that would imply a kind of pantheism: each of us would cease to exist, and Christ would be reduplicated throughout the Church. Rather, Paul is speaking in a figure, similar to Jesus' metaphor of the vine and the branches in John 14, in order to emphasize the intimacy of our union with Christ, who is the source from which we draw righteousness and holiness. Since our holiness is utterly dependent on Christ's, we have no ground for boasting except in the Lord.

2 Corinthians 5:21

> 21 God made him who had no sin to be sin for us, so that in him we might become the righteousness of God.

It is true that in "being sin" for us, Christ did not become internally sinful. The sinfulness he bore, he bore as a result of his solidarity with us, through assuming our human nature. This solidarity did require an internal modification of the Second Person: he could not have become sin for us without assuming an internal human nature. Similarly, we must take on, through an internal transformation by way of participation in Christ, the divine nature (as Peter teaches in 2 Peter 4:1).

Galatians 2:15–16

> 15 We who are Jews by birth and not "Gentile sinners" 16 know that a man is *not justified by observing the law, but by faith in Jesus Christ.* So we, too, have put our faith in Christ Jesus that we may be justified *by faith in Christ and not by observing the law,* because by observing the law no one will be justified.

The New International Version includes the unfortunate practice of rendering "works of the law" by "observing the law." As I mentioned above, Paul consistently uses "work" (*ergon*), and especially "work of the law" (*ergon nomou*), to refer to autonomous human actions that aim, apart from grace through faith, to secure a positive status before God.

Commentary on Proof Texts

Galatians 3:10–14

> 10 All who rely on observing the law are under a curse, for it is written: "Cursed is everyone who does not continue to do everything written in the Book of the Law." 11 Clearly no one is justified before God by the law, because, "The righteous will live by faith." 12 The law is not based on faith; on the contrary, "The man who does these things will live by them." 13 Christ redeemed us from the curse of the law by becoming a curse for us, for it is written: "Cursed is everyone who is hung on a tree." 14 He redeemed us in order that the blessing given to Abraham might come to the Gentiles through Christ Jesus, so that by faith we might receive the promise of the Spirit.

Throughout Galatians, Paul uses "the law" to refer specifically to the Law of Moses. This includes the moral law (the Ten Commandments), but it also includes all of the ritual and dietary regulations that separate Jews from Gentiles. The *curse of the law* is its propensity to separate Jews and Gentiles and to obscure the universality of Israel's God, making him appear to be a merely ethnic deity. Through his death on the cross, Jesus has destroyed that barrier that excludes the Gentiles from fellowship with him (Galatians 3:14) and that imprisons the Jews in false parochialism and ritualism (Galatians 4:3, 5).

Galatians 3:24–25

> 24 So the law was put in charge to lead us to Christ that we might be justified by faith. 25 Now that faith has come, we are no longer under the supervision of the law.

Paul again uses "the law" to refer to the Law of Moses, the old covenant whose binding force has lapsed once the promised Savior has come. The Law of Moses was never intended to be the means of individual salvation: to treat circumcision as essential for salvation or for inclusion in the Church is to set aside the unique work of Christ.

APPENDIX B

Galatians 5:4-6

> 4You who are trying to be justified by law have been alienated from Christ; you have fallen away from grace. 5But by faith we eagerly await through the Spirit the righteousness for which we hope. 6For in Christ Jesus neither circumcision nor uncircumcision has any value. The only thing that counts is faith expressing itself through love.

To treat circumcision as a matter of eternal significance is to deny the universality of the gospel of Christ, which God intends for the salvation of all men, Jews and Gentiles alike. Note that saving faith is a faith that "expresses itself" through love, i.e., a faith that is perpetually and effectively and internally active (*energeo*) through love.

Ephesians 2:8-10

> 8For it is by grace you have been saved, through faith—and this *not from yourselves*, it is the gift of God—9*not by works*, so that no one can boast. 10For we are God's workmanship, created in Christ Jesus to do good works, which God prepared in advance for us to do.

Faith in Christ is the channel through which we initially receive God's grace—Paul refers to our having been saved in the past (perfect tense), but it is not asserted that faith is the sole means by which we persist and grow in grace. The works that are excluded by verse 9 are those of the autonomous individual, prior to the reception of grace, since only such a person would have grounds for boasting. The good works the believer does (in which he "walks") after conversion are really the result of God's preparation, and so no grounds for boasting in oneself, however essential they are to one's growth in grace.

Commentary on Proof Texts

Philippians 3:8–9

> 8What is more, I consider everything a loss compared to the surpassing greatness of knowing Christ Jesus my Lord, for whose sake I have lost all things. I consider them rubbish, that I may gain Christ 9and be found in him, not having a righteousness of my own that comes from the law, but that which is through faith in Christ— the righteousness that comes from God and is by faith.

As in Galatians, the context of this passage indicates that Paul is using the phrase "the law" to refer to the Law of Moses. As Paul explains in many places, God never intended the Law of Moses to be the means for attaining individual righteousness (as opposed to national blessing). That righteousness is available only through faith in Christ.

Titus 3:4–7

> 4But when the kindness and love of God our Savior appeared, 5he saved us, *not because of righteous things we had done*, but because of his mercy. He saved us through the washing of *rebirth and renewal* by the Holy Spirit, 6whom he poured out on us generously through Jesus Christ our Savior, 7so that, having been justified by his grace, we might become heirs having the hope of eternal life.

As in Ephesians 2:8–9, Paul is referring to our having been saved at the point of our conversion. Conversion does not depend on any prior works or merit, as the Council of Trent explicitly affirmed. Note how closely justification by grace (in verse 7) is identified with rebirth and renewal by the Holy Spirit in verse 6. There is no shadow of the Protestant distinction between justification, regeneration, and sanctification here.

APPENDIX B

2 Timothy 1:9–10

> God, 9who has saved us and called us to a holy life—not because of anything we have done but because of his own purpose and grace. This grace was given us in Christ Jesus before the beginning of time, 10but it has now been revealed through the appearing of our Savior, Christ Jesus, who has destroyed death and has brought life and immortality to light through the gospel.

Once again, Paul is using "saved" to refer back to our conversion and rebirth, and denying that any prior actions on our part were prerequisites for our entrance into grace.

2 Timothy 3:15

> . . . 15and how from infancy you have known the holy Scriptures, which are able to make you wise for salvation through faith in Christ Jesus.

Here Paul is clearly referring to Timothy's future salvation, not his past conversion. Salvation is always "through" faith, since faith remains the root and foundation, not just the beginning of justification. However, Paul does not here state that salvation is through faith alone, to the exclusion of our growth in love and holiness. As the author of Hebrews states, it is impossible to please God without faith (Hebrews 11:14), and, as Paul himself states in Romans 14:23, whatever is not of faith is sin.

B. Other Texts

Matthew 25:37–39

> 37 Then the righteous will answer him, "Lord, when did we see you hungry and feed you, or thirsty and give you something to drink? 38When did we see you a stranger and invite you in, or needing clothes and clothe you?

Commentary on Proof Texts

> 39When did we see you sick or in prison and go to visit you?"

The saved are unaware of the fact that they have performed the works for which they are being rewarded. Their faith was focused exclusively on Christ; they did not rely on their own efforts, and their love for God and for others a natural outgrowth of that faith. Lutheran theologians are right to insist we must place our confidence in Christ and not in ourselves. However, it does not follow from this that there is, in fact, no connection between our works and the reward of eternal life. The works that please God are the fruit of the Holy Spirit in our lives. Their value is supernatural in nature, and as a result, no one can know which, if any, of his actions have this value or, if any do, to what degree. This is why the righteous must live by faith (Romans 1:17), trusting that God will produce through us works to which he will ascribe eternal value, graciously and for Christ's sake.

Mark 16:16

> 16Whoever believes and is baptized will be saved, but whoever does not believe will be condemned.

This, and similar passages, refer to baptism and conversion as the sufficient means for entering into a state of grace. Lutherans do not think that all who are baptized and believe are among the elect, since only those who persevere in saving faith will enter into eternal life.

Luke 18:9-14

> 9To some who were confident of their own righteousness and looked down on everybody else, Jesus told this parable: 10 "Two men went up to the temple to pray, one a Pharisee and the other a tax collector. 11The Pharisee stood up and prayed about himself: 'God, I thank you

that I am not like other men—robbers, evildoers, adulterers—or even like this tax collector. 12I fast twice a week and give a tenth of all I get.'

13 "But the tax collector stood at a distance. He would not even look up to heaven, but beat his breast and said, 'God, have mercy on me, a sinner.'

14 "I tell you that this man, rather than the other, went home justified before God. For everyone who exalts himself will be humbled, and he who humbles himself will be exalted."

To rely upon one's own righteous deeds, and to be blind to one's sins, is not to be in a state of grace. Humility is a crucial virtue. There is nothing in this passage to suggest that the tax collector's justification was wholly external in character.

Lutherans argue that Roman Catholic theology faces here an inescapable dilemma: since it ascribes a role to human works in securing salvation, it must either commend the Pharisee for his self-confidence, or drive the tax collector to despair. Where, after all, is the Pharisee's error? He piously attributes his righteous deeds to God by thanking God that he is as he is.

The Pharisee's error is twofold: he overlooks his own sin and need for divine forgiveness and mercy (1 John 1:8), and he wrongly believes that he can assess the merits of his life through reflection and introspection. In fact, only God can judge what acts merit eternal life, because only he knows which acts are genuinely the fruit of the Spirit. (See 1 Corinthians 4:4.)

Lutherans are right to see a danger in pastoral practice here: the Pharisee needs to hear the law, to puncture his complacent self-confidence, and the tax collector needs to hear the pure and unconditional promises of the gospel. The comfortable need to be afflicted, and the afflicted, comforted. However, Lutherans are wrong in thinking that the correct soteriology (theory of salvation) will guarantee good pastoral practice. We can readily imagine a "Lutheran Pharisee," who smugly thanks God that he is not like other men, formulaically despairing of his own righteousness and trusting only in Christ, and a "Lutheran tax collector" who turns to God, confessing his own self-righteousness and lack of faith. Surely it is the latter, rather than the former, who returns home justified, despite the former's scrupulously correct Evangelical theology.

Conversely, a Roman Catholic soteriology does not inevitably lead to bad pastoral practice. Self-righteousness remains a mortal sin, even if disguised as thanksgiving for God's grace, and a humble contrition should be met with a tender offer of mercy, even if the supernatural fruit of this repentance plays a role in meriting eternal life.

Acts 13:39

> 39 Through him everyone who believes is justified from everything you could not be justified from by the law of Moses.

This early proclamation of Paul's, recorded in Acts, clearly brings out the fact that faith justifies because it connects us with the Christ's New Covenant, in contrast with the way of life prescribed by the Law of Moses, which was incapable of bringing about such justification. Thus, it is the works of the Torah that are excluded, not all human action, without exception.

John 3:16

> 16 For God so loved the world that he gave his one and only Son, that whoever believes in him shall not perish but have eternal life.

The second clause indicates that it is God's purpose, in sending his Son, to bring all believers to eternal life. This does not say that nothing but faith is needed for this purpose to be realized. Certainly, it is normal for faith to lead effectively to eternal life, since faith opens the door to the abundance of God's grace and help.

APPENDIX B

1 Peter 1:8-9

> 8Though you have not seen him, you love him; and even though you do not see him now, you believe in him and are filled with an inexpressible and glorious joy, 9for you are receiving the goal of your faith, the salvation of your souls.

This confirms that the purpose or end (*telos*) of faith is the salvation of our souls. This salvation is something that the believer is continually receiving, in the form of fresh infusions of God's transforming grace.

II. Roman Catholic Proof Texts

A. Justification includes Sanctification: Not Merely Forensic

Galatians 6:15

> 15Neither circumcision nor uncircumcision means anything; what counts is a new creation.

Paul teaches that it is the new creation, not the imputation of an alien righteousness, that ultimately "counts." This new creation is the transformation of the believer through grace into a new state of spiritual life, a life infused by faith, hope, and love.

Philippians 2:12-13

> 12Therefore, my dear friends, as you have always obeyed—not only in my presence, but now much more in my absence—continue to work out your salvation with fear and trembling, 13for it is God who works in you to will and to act according to his good purpose.

Commentary on Proof Texts

Lutheran theology is based on a series of false dilemmas: either Christ's merits or my merits, either God's doing or my doing, either Christ's righteousness or my righteousness. In this passage, Paul clearly rejects such dilemmas: we are to work out our own salvation, and yet our doing so is also wholly God's work within us. This is why it is consistent to say that our salvation is due, 100 percent, to God's grace, and yet also depends on our continuing cooperation.

Moreover, this working we are to do is to be "with fear and trembling," not with a complacency grounded in the mistaken idea that everything that's needed for my salvation has already been done.

2 Thessalonians 2:13

> 13But we ought always to thank God for you, brothers loved by the Lord, because from the beginning God chose you to be saved through the *sanctifying* work of the Spirit and through belief in the truth.

We are saved, not only by the imputation of Christ's righteousness and the forgiveness of sins, but also by the sanctifying work of the Spirit. Justification may be a forensic concept, but sanctification is a simple, causative one: to sanctify is to make holy.

1 Corinthians 6:11

> 11And that is what some of you were. But you were washed, you were *sanctified*, you were justified in the name of the Lord Jesus Christ and by the Spirit of our God.

This verse again belies a simplistic distinction between justification and sanctification. Paul refers to them as a real unity, effected by our baptism.

APPENDIX B

Hebrews 13:12

12And so Jesus also suffered outside the city gate to *make the people holy* through his own blood.

The effect of Christ's passion is to make us holy, not merely to impute his holiness to us.

I Peter 1:1-2

1Peter, an apostle of Jesus Christ,

To God's elect, strangers in the world, scattered throughout Pontus, Galatia, Cappadocia, Asia and Bithynia, 2who have been chosen according to the foreknowledge of God the Father, through the *sanctifying* work of the Spirit, for *obedience* to Jesus Christ and sprinkling by his blood:

Grace and peace be yours in abundance.

Our election is brought about by the sanctifying work of the Spirit, producing within us a state of real obedience to Christ. This is not consistent with justification being an external status communicated to us by faith alone.

Acts 26:17-18

17I will rescue you from your own people and from the Gentiles. I am sending you to them 18to open their eyes and turn them from darkness to light, and from the power of Satan to God, so that they may receive forgiveness of sins and a place among those who are *sanctified* by faith in me.

Forgiveness of sins is tied to sanctification through faith.

Commentary on Proof Texts

Hebrews 10:10, 13–14

> 10And by that will, we *have been made holy* through the sacrifice of the body of Jesus Christ once for all.

> 13Since that time he waits for his enemies to be made his footstool, 14because by one sacrifice he has *made perfect* forever those who are *being made holy*.

Note in verse 14 that Christ "has perfected" (perfect past tense) those who "are being sanctified" (present tense). This is a paradoxical statement, since if someone has already been perfected, what room is there for further sanctification? The solution lies in taking into account the fact that God transcends the limitations of time. Consequently, the final state (the *eschaton*) is both realized already and to be realized in the future.

The saved are made perfect forever by Christ's sacrifice, but this perfection is also gradually realized through the process of sanctification. The two are inseparable: Christ has not made perfect (in eternity) those whom he is not now sanctifying (in time). Hence, it is completed sanctification, and not merely a static condition of faith, that is required for salvation.

B. The Sanctified Fulfill the Law

Romans 8:4

> ... 4in order that the righteous requirements of the law might be fully met in us, who do not live according to the sinful nature but according to the Spirit.

Galatians 5:18

> 18But if you are led by the Spirit, you are not under law.

Note that we are not under the law, *not* because we have an external, alien righteousness, but because we are (internally) being led by the Spirit.

Galatians 5:22–23

> 22But the fruit of the Spirit is love, joy, peace, patience, kindness, goodness, faithfulness, 23gentleness and self-control. Against such things there is no law.

In both Romans and Galatians, Paul avoids anti-nomianism, the setting aside or nullification of the moral law. Instead, the new life in the Spirit makes possible for the believer in Christ a life that fully accords with the moral content of the law.

C. Rewards Based on Good Works

Romans 2:6–8

> 6God "will give to each person according to what he has done." 7To those *who by persistence in doing good* seek glory, honor and immortality, he will give eternal life. 8But for those who are self-seeking and who reject the truth and follow evil, there will be wrath and anger.

Galatians 6:8

> 8The one who sows to please his sinful nature, from that nature will reap destruction; the one *who sows to please the Spirit*, from the Spirit will reap eternal life.

Our everyday choices as Christians have eternal consequences. If we choose to resist and grieve the Spirit, we can lose the state of grace and face eternal damnation. Conversely, our willing cooperation with the Spirit is essential to our obtaining eternal bliss.

COMMENTARY ON PROOF TEXTS

2 Timothy 4:8

8Now there is in store for me the crown of righteousness, which the Lord, the righteous Judge, will award to me on that day—and not only to me, but also to all *who have longed for his appearing.*

The Greek reads "to those who have loved (*agapao*) his appearing." Paul speaks of the crown of righteousness as a reward for our love of Christ.

James 1:12

12Blessed is the man who perseveres under trial, because when he has stood the test, he will receive the crown of life that God has promised to those *who love him.*

Like Paul, James makes our love of God the basis of the reward of eternal life. We are justified by faith, but not to the exclusion of love.

James 2:14, 21–24

14What good is it, my brothers, if a man claims to have faith but has no deeds? Can such faith save him?

21Was not our ancestor Abraham considered righteous for what he did when he offered his son Isaac on the altar? 22You see that his faith and his actions were working together, and his faith was made complete by what he did. 23And the scripture was fulfilled that says, "Abraham believed God, and it was credited to him as righteousness," and he was called God's friend. 24You see that a person is justified by what he does and not by faith alone.

Lutherans can legitimately point out that, in this passage, James uses "faith" to refer merely to what Lutherans call "historical knowledge" (intellectual assent to certain propositions) and not to saving faith (real trust in Christ as one's savior). In fact, James seems to have in mind by "faith" merely the knowledge that God exists ("you believe that God is one," James 2:19), not even the knowledge that Christ is divine. However, what creates problems for Lutherans is not the phrase "not by faith alone" but the phrase "justified by what he does." To reconcile this with Lutheran doctrine, Lutherans must argue that by "justification" James means not justification before God but justification before people and angels (either in this life or at the final judgment).

This is David Scaer's argument in *James*:

> James addresses the question of how the righteous are identifiable *in the world*. For Paul the question is: How do I know that I am justified? For James the question is: How does *the world* know I am justified? Abraham was accepted as righteous before God through faith (Paul), but he was recognized as righteous *to the world and to the succession of believers for all time* through his willing obedience to sacrifice his son Isaac at God's command (James). Paul and James are speaking to the same forensic reality in which the believer appears before God as the Judge. The believer through faith accepts Christ's righteousness as his own and is viewed by God as righteous (Paul). By works the Christian vindicates God's verdict of righteousness by demonstrating *to the world* (emphasis mine) the correctness of that verdict (James).[2]

There is little in the context to suggest this reading. In verse 14, James raises the question of what "saves" us, and in verses 22 and 23 James states that Abraham's works "perfected" his faith, and that it was this works-perfected faith that God reckoned to be righteousness. Thus, it is individual salvation and righteousness before God that are in view in this passage. Indeed, Scaer himself admits that "Paul and James are speaking to the same forensic reality in which the believer appears before God as judge." Scaer's claim that works play a role merely in justifying the believer (or

2. Scaer, *James*, 93.

Commentary on Proof Texts

God's verdict) before men is without any basis whatsoever in the text. Although James does refer to "showing" one's faith with or without works to another, he doesn't identify this "showing" with justification, nor does he explicitly exclude being justified before God from the "justification" that is from works. The last judgment is simultaneously a vindication of the righteous both before God and before people and angels. There is no biblical warrant for separating the two. Moreover, if our faith is sufficient to justify us before God, apart from works, how could it fail to justify us before men? Are human standards higher than God's? We are told that at the judgment day, all of the secret motives of men's hearts will be disclosed (1 Corinthians 4:5), so why would external evidence of faith be needed then?

The word "saves" in verse 14 is in the future tense, which fits perfectly the Roman Catholic view: faith is the root and beginning of justification, but works are needed to fulfill faith's purpose and bring us to glory (works "complete" or "perfect" faith, as James says in verse 22).

Scaer attempts another reconciliation by arguing that James is teaching that we are justified out of (Greek *ek*) works, while Paul teaches that we are justified through (Greek *dia*) faith alone. This is simply a slip on Scaer's part, however, since Paul very commonly speak of our being justified out of (*ek*) faith and not works: Romans 1:17; 3:26, 30; 4:16; 5:1; 10:6; 14:23; Galatians 2:16; 3:7–9, 11–12, 22, 24; 5:5. In any case, to say that our justification *springs or arises from* our works, while faith is merely the instrument *through which* we are justified, seems to favor the Roman Catholic rather than the Lutheran theory.

It is true that there is no contradiction between Paul and James. It is striking that they both appeal to the very same verse about Abraham's faith being reckoned for righteousness from Genesis 15. However, there is a much more natural synthesis of the two than the "double justification" proposed by Scaer and other Lutherans, namely, that Paul and James mean different things by "works." By works, Paul means works performed under a system of law, in which the unredeemed seeks to use the letter of the law to impose a legal obligation on God. James has a much wider sense in mind, one that includes what Paul would describe as the fruit of walking in Christ's Spirit. James very clearly has in mind works as the fruit and expression of faith (here, both Lutherans and Roman Catholics are fully in agreement). The only question is: do such works justify us before God? The most natural reading of James suggests that they do, and I have not found any warrant in Paul's epistles for thinking that they do not.

Revelation 22:12

12Behold, I am coming soon! My reward is with me, and I will give to everyone *according to what he has done*.

APPENDIX C

St. Augustine's *On the Spirit and the Letter* on Justification as Inherent Righteousness

> He does not, indeed, extend His mercy to them because they know Him, but that they may know Him; nor is it because they are upright in heart, but *that they may become so*, that He extends to them His righteousness, whereby he justifies the ungodly. (Chapter 11, p. 87)

God justifies us by extending to us his righteousness, making us upright in heart.

> His words are, "The righteousness of God is manifested:" [Romans 3:21] he does not say, the righteousness of man, or the righteousness of his own will, but the "righteousness of God,"—not that by whereby He Himself is righteous, but that with which He endows man when He justifies the ungodly.... It is not, therefore, by the law, nor is it by their own will, that they are justified; but they are justified freely by His grace,—not that it is wrought without our will; but our will is by the law shown to be weak, that *grace may heal its infirmity; and that our healed will may fulfill the law*, not by compact under the law, *nor yet in the absence of law*. (Chapter 13, p. 89)

1. From St. Augustine, *Anti-Pelagian Writings: Nicene and Post-Nicene Fathers of the Christian Church*, vol. 5.

APPENDIX C

We are justified by a grace that is infused into us, healing our wills and enabling us to fulfill the law. We are not justified under the law, but neither are we justified in the absence of or apart from law.

> Now it is freely that he is justified thereby [by grace],—that is, on account of no *antecedent* merit of his own works; "otherwise grace is no more grace" [Galatians 3:24], since it is bestowed on us, *not because we have done good works, but that we may be able to do them*,—in other words, not because we have fulfilled the law, but in order that we may be able to fulfill the law . . . for it is not by the law that he becomes righteous, but by the law of faith, which led him to believe that no other resource was possible to his weakness for fulfilling the precepts which "the law of works" commanded, except to be assisted by the grace of God. (Chapter 16, p. 90)

Augustine interprets Paul (in the epistle to the Galatians) to be excluding from salvation the *antecedent* merit of our works: that is, any merit pertaining to works performed prior to the infusion of God's grace. When God's grace heals our will and enables us to fulfill the law, our works (assisted by grace) do then have merit.

> . . . by the law of faith, not by the law of works, this boasting was excluded, in the other sense of shut out and driven away; because by the law of faith every one learns that whatever good life he leads he has from the grace of God, and that from no other source whatever can he obtain the means of becoming perfect in the love of righteousness. (Chapter 17, p. 90)

Boasting is excluded, not because our works have no role to play in meriting salvation, but because those works are due entirely to the grace of God.

> . . . it is called the righteousness of God, because *by His bestowal of it He makes us righteous*, just as we read that "salvation is the Lord's," because He makes us safe. . . . By this faith of Jesus Christ—that is, the faith which Christ has given us—we believe it is from God that we now

> have, and shall have more and more, *the ability of living righteously*; wherefore we give Him thanks ... (Chapter 18, p. 90)

Justification is a matter of our being made (not merely being imputed to be) righteous.

> What the law of works enjoins by menace, that the law of faith secures by faith ... Accordingly, by the law of works, God says to us, Do what I command thee; but by the law of faith we say to God, Give me what Thou commandest ... if he has at once the ability, and complies with the command, he ought also to be aware from whose gift the ability comes ... Let him not fall into the mistake of the Pharisee, who, while thanking God for what he possessed, yet failed to ask for any further gift, just as if he stood in want of nothing for the increase and perfection of his righteousness. (Chapter 22, pp. 92–93)

The Pharisee's error did not lie in seeing works as meritorious, but in foolishly believing that he was in need of no further grace.

> There the law was given outwardly, so that the unrighteous might be terrified; here it was given inwardly, that they might be justified. (Chapter 29, p. 95)

Augustine identifies justification with the Spirit's making God's law internal to our hearts.

> It is not by their works, but by grace, that the doers of the Law are justified.
>
> Now he could not mean to contradict himself in saying, "The doers of the law shall be justified," as if their justification came through their works, and not through grace; since he declares that a man is justified freely by His grace, without the works of the law, (Romans 3:24, 28) intending by the term "freely" nothing else than *that works do not precede justification* ... Justification does not subsequently accrue to them as doers of the law, but justification precedes them as doers of the law—by Him,

of course, who justifies the ungodly man, that he may become a godly one instead ... And thus it amounts to the same thing as if it were said, The doers of the Law shall be created,—not those who were so already, but that they may become such; in order that the Jews who were hearers of the Law might thereby understand that they wanted the grace of the Justifier, in order to be able to become its doers also. (Chapter 45, p. 102)

Augustine interprets Romans 3 as excluding only those works that precede justification, not those that follow from it. Justification consists in our being made "doers of the law."

Belonging to the new testament means having the law of God not written on tables, but on the heart,—that is, *embracing the righteousness of the law with innermost affection, where faith works by love* [Galatians 5:6]. (Chapter 46)

But Israel, which followed after the law of righteousness, hath not attained to the law of righteousness. And why? Because they sought it not by faith, but as it were by works—in other words, working it out as it were by themselves, not believing that it is God who works within them [Philippians 2:13]. (Chapter 50, p. 105)

Israel's error lies, not in relying on works per se, but only on relying on works without believing that those works are the result of God's grace working within.

As far as he is saved, so far is he righteous. For by this faith we believe that God will raise even us from the dead,—even now in the spirit, that we may in this present world live soberly, righteously, and godly in the renewal of His grace; and by and by in our flesh, which shall raise again to immortality, which indeed is the reward of the Spirit, who precedes it by a resurrection that is appropriate to Himself,—that is, by justification. (Chapter 51, p. 105)

Augustine identifies justification with regeneration in the Spirit.

> Accordingly, as the law is not made void, but is established through faith, since *faith procures grace whereby the law is fulfilled*; so free will is not made void through grace, but is established, since *grace cures the will whereby righteousness is freely loved* . . . (Chapter 52)

The grace that faith procures is that infused grace by which the will is healed.

Bibliography

Augustine. *Anti-Pelagian Writings: Nicene and Post-Nicene Fathers of the Christian Church*, vol. 5. Edited by Phillip Schaff. Translated by Peter Holmes, Robert Ernest Wallis, and Benjamin B. Warfield. New York: Scribner's Sons, 1908.
———. *Enchiridion on Faith, Hope, and Charity*. Edited by Henry Paolucci. Chicago: Henry Regnery, 1961.
———. "Letter 186 to Paulinus." In *The Faith of the Early Fathers*, edited by W. A. Jurgens, vol. 3, 10. Collegeville, MN: Liturgical, 1970-79.
Balduin, Friedrich. *Commentarius in omnis Epistulas Beati Apostoli Pauli*. Frankfurt am Main: Ex officina Zumnneriana, typis Johannis Philippi Andreae, 1710.
Bellarmine, Robert. *Disputations about the Controversies of the Christian Faith*. Translated by Peter L. P. Simpson. http://www.aristotelophile.com/current.htm.
The Book of Concord (the Lutheran Confessions). St. Louis: Concordia, 1922. www.bookofconcord.org.
Braaten, C. E., and R. W. Jenson. *Union with Christ: The New Finnish Interpretation of Luther*. Grand Rapids: Eerdmans, 1998.
The Catechism of the Catholic Church. United States Catholic Conference, Inc. San Francisco: Ignatius, 1994. See also www.usccb.org/catechism/text/.
Chemnitz, Martin. *Examination of the Council of Trent, Part I*. Translated by Fred Kramer. St. Louis: Concordia, 1971.
———. *Justification: The Chief Article of Christian Doctrine as Expounded in the Loci Theologici*. Translated by J. A. O. Preus. St. Louis: Concordia, 1985.
Chrysostom, John. *On Repentance and Almsgiving*. Translated by Gus George Christo. Washington, DC: Catholic University of America Press, 1998.
The Council of Trent. history.hanover.edu/texts/trent/.
Dunn, James D. G. *The New Perspective on Paul*. Minneapolis: Fortress, 2005.
Geisler, Norman L., and Ralph E. MacKenzie. *Roman Catholics and Evangelicals: Agreements and Differences*. Grand Rapids: Baker, 1995.
Joint Declaration on the Doctrine of Justification. http://www.cin.org/users/james/files/jddj.htm.

BIBLIOGRAPHY

Lewis, C. S. *The Great Divorce*. New York: Macmillan, 1946.
Lindbeck, George A. *The Nature of Doctrine: Religion and Theology in a Postliberal Age*. Philadelphia: Westminster, 1984.
Luther, Martin. "Disputation on Justification." In *Luther's Works*, vol. 34: Career of the Reformer IV, translated by Lewis W. Spitz, 145–96. Philadelphia: Muhlenberg, 1960.
———. "Lectures on the Epistle to the Galatians (1535)." *Luther's Works*, vol. 26. Edited by J. Pelikan. St. Louis: Concordia, 1963.
———. *Luther's Works*, vol. 4. Edited by J. Pelikan. St. Louis: Concordia, 1955.
———. *Luther's Works*, vol. 40. Edited by J. Pelikan. St. Louis: Concordia, 1963.
———. *Luther's Works*, vol. 51. Edited by J. Pelikan. St. Louis: Concordia, 1955.
———. *On the Bondage of the Will*. Translated by J. I. Packer and O. R. Johnson Westwood, NJ: Revell, 1957.
———. "Sermon for the Feast of the Beheading of John the Baptist (1532)." In *Dr. M. Luthers Sämmtliche Werke*, vol. 6, 281–82. Frankfurt am Main und Erlangen: Verlag Heyder und Zimmer, 1826–1857.
Malloy, Christopher J. *Engrafted into Christ: A Critique of the Joint Declaration*. New York: Peter Lang, 2005.
McGrath, Alister E. *Iustitia Dei: A History of the Doctrine of Justification*. 3rd ed. Cambridge: Cambridge University Press, 2005.
———. *Justitia Dei: A History of the Christian Doctrine of Justification*. Cambridge: Cambridge University Press, 1998.
Melanchthon, Phillip. *Apology of the Augsburg Confession*. St. Louis: Concordia, 1922.
Newman, John Henry. *An Essay on the Development of Doctrine*. Edited by Charles F. Harrold. New York: Longman, Green, and Co., 1949.
Oden, Thomas C. *The Justification Reader*. Grand Rapids: Eerdmans, 2002.
Origen. *Commentary on the Epistle to the Romans*. Translated by Thomas P. Scheck. Washington, DC: Catholic University of America Press, 2001.
Preus, Robert. *The Inspiration of Scripture: A Study in the Theology of 17th Century Lutheran Dogmaticians*. Edinburgh: Oliver and Boyd, 1955.
———. *Justification and Rome*. St. Louis: Concordia, 1997.
Quenstedt, Johann Andreas. *Theologia Didactico-Polemica Sive Systema Theologicum*. Leipzig: Thomam Fritsch, 1715.
Roberts, Alexander, and James Donaldson, eds. *Ante-Nicene Christian Library: Translations of the Writings of the Fathers down to AD 325*. Edinburgh: T. and T. Clark, 1867.
Sanders, E. P. *Paul and Palestinian Judaism*. Minneapolis: Fortress, 1977.
Scaer, David P. *James: The Apostle of Faith*. Eugene, OR: Wipf and Stock, 1994.
Walther, C. F. W. *The Proper Distinction between Law and Gospel: Thirty-Nine Evening Lectures*. St. Louis: Concordia, 1929.
Wright, N. T. *Paul: In Fresh Perspective*. Minneapolis: Fortress, 2005.
———. *What St. Paul Really Said*. Grand Rapids: Eerdmans, 1997.
Zetterholm, Magnus. *Approaches to Paul: A Student's Guide to Recent Scholarship*. Minneapolis: Fortress, 2009.

Scripture Index

Gen.
15 — 119, 139

Deut.
18:19–20 — 72
30:11–14 — 64
2 Sam. 12 — 104

Psalm
119 — 64

Prov.
6:23 — 64

Jeremiah
— 8

Matt.
10:28 — 109
15:8–9 — 62
16:18 — 83
18:20 — 72
24:13 — 12
25:31–46 — 41, 128–29
28:20 — 8

Mark
16:16 — 12, 129

Luke
1:28 — 78–79
8:9–14 — 129–31
12:5 — 109
16:29 — 63
23:43 — 21
24:27 — 63

John
3:16 — 12, 131–32
5:39–46 — 63, 72
14:13–14 — 72
14:26 — 8
15:12 — 9
16:13 — 66
17:19 — 9
17:21–23 — 9

Acts
4:1–8 — 106, 111
13:39 — 131
14:23 — 70
14:26 — 22
16:13 — 82
17:17–19 — 96
17:21 — 8

Scripture Index

Acts (*continued*)

20:17	70
20:27	62
20:32	22
21:15–17	83
26:17–18	21, 96, 115, 134–35

Romans

1:5	22
1:17	128–29, 139
2:6–11	12, 30, 41, 115, 120, 136
3	25
3:20	23
3:21–31	22, 24, 26–27, 31, 117–19, 139, 143
4	25
4:2–9	22, 26–27, 38, 119–21
4:16	121–22, 139
5:1–2	30, 122–23, 139
5:5	111, 115
5:17	122–23
5:20, 21	22
6:1	22
6:4	89
6:14–5	22
7:7	23
7:25	21
8:1–17	21, 23, 30, 45, 89, 102, 115, 135
9	8
10:6	139
10:8	64
10:9	123
11:5,6	22, 26
12:3,6	22
14:23	10, 139

1 Corinthians

1:30–31	36, 123–24
3:15	21
4:4	130
4:5	139
6:9	45
6:10	115
6:11	21, 42, 96, 133–34
9:24	42
10:12	46
11:2	65

2 Corinthians

1:15	22
5:20	78
5:21	36, 124
8:4, 6–7	22
12:9	22

Galatians

1:2	96
1:6	22
2:9	22
2:15–16	124, 139
2:20–22	22, 102, 115
3	25
3:7–14	125, 139
3:15	21
3:17	23
3:22–25	125, 142, 139
5:4–6	110, 115, 126, 139, 143
5:16–25	21, 23, 41, 45, 115, 136
6:7–8	21, 41, 136
6:15	115, 132–33

Ephesians

1:7	22
2:7–10	19, 22, 27, 120, 126

2:16	27	**Titus**	
2:20	36, 39	1:5	70
3:8	22	3:4–7	22, 27, 96, 127
3:11	27		
4:7, 29	22, 27	**Hebrews**	
4:22–24	89	3:12	46
4:29	22, 27	4:16	22
5:4	45	10:10	96, 135
6:8	30	10:13–14	20–21, 115, 135
		10:35	42

Philippians

2:12–13	46, 51, 143	11:6	42–43, 98
3:8–9	27, 36, 127	11:14	128
3:14	42	12:1	77
		12:15	22

Colossians

3	90	13:7	7
3:6	45	13:9	22
3:9–10	89	13:12	21, 96, 134
3:24	42		

James

		8

2 Thessalonians

2:13	21, 96, 115	1:2	137
2:16	22	1:12	42
3:13	133	1:25	33
		2:14,	137–38
		2:21–24	25, 115, 137–38

1 Timothy

2:2	66	4:6	22
3:2	70	5:16	76
3:15	66, 70		

1 Peter

1:1–2	21, 96, 115, 134

2 Timothy

1	27	1:8–9	109, 132
1:9–10	22, 26–27, 128	1:13	22
1:13	66	2:9	78
2:1	22	2:20	22
2:2	71	3:17	46
2:5	89	4:10	22
3:15	128	5:5	22
3:16–17	62		
4:8	42, 115, 137		

2 Peter

1:10	25, 41, 44, 50, 57, 115
1:19	64
3:18	22
4:1	124

1 John

1:8	130
1:9	90
5:14–15	72

Jude

3	66
4	22

Revelation

6:10	77
8:3–4	77
11:18	42
20:12–15	41
22:12	42, 115, 140

General Index

Abraham 119, 122, 137–38
absolution 39, 47, 51, 52n33, 53,
    55, 80, 102–4, 113
acceptance by God 11, 26,
adoption 14, 49, 55, 93, 97
Ambrose 2
Ambrosiaster 5
Apology of the Augsburg
    Confession 3n5, 18n11,
    23n16, 42, 44, 76, 106,
    110
apostolic succession 7, 9, 70–71
Aquinas, Thomas x, 32, 38, 54,
Arianism 7
Aristotle 32, 96
assurance of salvation – see
    salvation, assurance of
Augsburg Confession 77
Augustine 2, 3, 5, 14, 23, 25, 27,
    115, 141–45
autonomy 23, 28, 126,

Balduin, Friedrich 15
baptism 6, 13, 40, 47, 89, 123
    infant 7–8, 52n32, 60–61, 67
Basil of Caesarea 2
Bellarmine, Robert 62n1
Biel, Gabriel 39, 54, 95
bishops – see *episcopacy*
boasting 33, 36, 124, 126, 142

Bondage of the Will 91–92,
    107–8, 111, 114
Book of Concord 19, 30n17, 64
Braaten, C. E. 20n13

Calvin, John 79, 93, 107
Calvinism 44, 57
canon of Scripture – see
    Scripture, canon of
Catechism of the Catholic Church
    xiii, 17, 33n22, 36n24,
    38, 39n25, 55–56, 80n3
charity 24, 26, 53, 56, 99, 110,
    115–16, 137
    of Christ 17, 56
Chemnitz, Martin 3, 54–55
Christ
    as mediator 42–43, 54, 78
    as Savior 29, 78, 114, 138
    death of 25–26, 40, 43
    life of 24
    merits of 1, 36–37, 42, 49,
        55–57, 94, 98, 105, 133
    righteousness of 2, 12, 16,
        31, 36, 39, 97, 111, 114,
        120
    sacrifice of 48, 80, 135
christocentricity 36
Chrystostom, John 2, 5–6
Church discipline 9, 47
Church Fathers 1, 4–5, 7, 25, 63

General Index

Church, identity of true, 68–70
  unity of xi, 6, 8–9, 61, 64, 70, 72, 81–85
circumcision 22–23, 26–29, 118, 125–26, 132
Clement of Rome 2
Commentary on Galatians (1535) 15
communion with God 57–58, 98
Communion, Holy 34, 39, 52n34, 68, 81, 101
Concord, Book of – see *Book of Concord*
confession – see *Reconciliation; absolution*
conversion 24, 26, 29, 126, 128
cooperation with grace 20, 24, 45–46, 76, 79, 94, 133, 136; see also *monergism*
Council of Trent 19n12
Councils xiii, 7, 9, 59–60, 64–65
credit (*logizomai*) 119, 121
creeds, ecumenical 61, 64
Cyprian 1, 71

damnation 54, 92n1, 108, 136
deductivist method 67
discipline, fatherly 47–48, 76, 90, 104
Disputation on Justification 15
doctrines, essential 63–64, 68–69
Donatism 52n34
Dunn, James D. G. 22n15

earning salvation xiii, 13, 38, 49, 118
Eastern Orthodox churches 69, 82–84
election 51, 102, 108, 115
engrafting in Christ 15, 97
episcopacy x, 60, 70–73, 83
Essay on the Development of Doctrine ix, 7, 60, 83

eternal life 30, 39, 105, 129, 131
Eucharist 8, 9, 52n33, 80–81
  Real Presence in 80–81
evangelicals, American 44, 98
ex opera operata 52–53, 112–13,
Examination of the Council of Trent 54
excommunication 7n14, 73n5
extra nos 2, 16, 56, 114

faith 10, 11, 16, 26
  as a work 29
  as intellectual assent 29, 105, 138
  as receptivity 26, 30–31
  as trust 29, 105, 110, 112, 114
  working through love 2, 25, 36, 110, 126
  as root of justification 19, 43, 57, 109, 128, 131–32
  saving 29, 45, 51–53, 98, 138
  virtue of 11, 22, 24, 29, 32, 36, 97
Fathers, Church –see *Church Fathers*
forgiveness 5–6, 10, 29, 33, 36–37, 39, 42, 47, 52n33, 53–5, 90, 97, 101–4, 112–13, 121, 133–35
formal cause 36, 97, 99, 123
Formula of Concord, 19, 30n17, 33n21, 34, 45, 51, 92, 107
fragmentation of the Church 6
fruit of the Spirit 23–24, 30, 50, 56, 102, 106

Geisler, Norman L. 13n1
Gentile and Jew 23, 28, 29, 122, 126
glorification 20, 57
Gnosticism 7, 20
good works 40, 41, 56, 81

General Index

Gospel and Law – see *Law and Gospel*
Gospel xii
   as good news 35
   as new law, 33, 34
   grace 10, 11, 26, 42, 122, 126,
grace
   cooperation with 20, 24, 33, 45–46, 76, 79, 94, 110, 116, 118, 122, 133, 136
   favor vs. help 22, 28, 57
   increase of 38, 39, 101, 116, 132
   infusion of 14, 24, 26, 29, 39, 53, 96, 99, 105, 110, 116, 120, 142, 145
   irresistible 107
   means of 39, 44, 57, 101–2
   state of 51–52
guilt 46

Heidelberg Disputation against Scholastic Philosophy 92, 108
hermeneutics 25, 53
historical continuity x
Holy Spirit 8, 15, 24, 45, 57, 62, 66–68, 85, 92–98, 102–3, 106–7, 110–12, 114, 118, 120, 122, 127, 129, 133–36, 140, 144,
   fellowship of 49
Honorius I, Pope 64
hope 11, 24, 26, 29, 31–3, 96–97, 107, 109–10, 115–16, 119, 127

Ignatius 70
imputation 13–14, 18; see also *righteousness, imputed*
indwelling of Christ, 15
indwelling of the Spirit 112

infant baptism – see *baptism, infant*
infusion – see *grace, infusion of*
innovation ix; see also *novelty*
Irenaeus 71

James 26, 138–40
Jenson, Robert W. 20n13
Jerome 5, 23, 118
Jesus, teaching of 24, 26
Joint Declaration on Justification xi
judgment of God 49, 54–55, 104, 109, 138–39
justification – see also *righteousness*
   as forensic 14–15, 91, 119, 121
   by faith alone 2–4, 11, 31, 46, 56, 109, 114, 138
   by works 36, 138, 144,
   first 15, 39
   doctrine of xi, xii, 7, 10
   faith as root of – see *faith as root of justification*
   formal cause of 36, 97, 99, 123
   fruits of 18
   law-based 29
   meritorious cause of 36, 97, 114
   objective 36, 55, 57
   subjective condition of 30, 32, 37, 40, 55
   vs. sanctification 21, 95, 102, 127, 133–35, 143

Large Catechism, Luther's 8, 60
Law and Gospel, 33, 35
Law
   as mirror 29
   condemnation by 54
   fulfilling of 29, 102, 135–36, 141, 144

Old Testament 22–23, 26, 33, 34, 91, 118, 122, 125, 127, 131
  third use of 45
  work of 23, 25, 26, 27, 28, 29, 120–21, 124, 140
Leo X, 6n13
Lewis, C. S. 57, 79
Lindbeck, George A. 53
logical contradiction 46
losing salvation – see *salvation, loss of*
love of God 29
love—see *charity*
Luther, Martin 8, 14, 16, 25, 36, 60, 78n2, 79, 92, 94, 107–8, 111, 114
Lutheran Confessions 8; see also *Book of Concord*

MacKenzie, Ralph 13n2
magisterium 59, 61, 68, 73
Malloy, Christopher J. 96
Marcion 67
marriage 17
Mary 49, 60, 77–80
Mass, sacrifice of the 80–81
McGrath, Alister 13, 20n13
Melanchthon, Phillip 3, 18n11, 23n16, 42–44; 76, 106, 110, 119
merit xiii, 12–13, 33, 38–39, 44, 56, 81, 97
  absolute 38
  an increase of grace 38, 116
  as grace 33
  causal vs. forensic role 13, 39
  condign 13, 38
  congruous 38
meritorious cause – see *justification, meritorious cause of*
merits of Christ – see *Christ, merits of*

merits, supernatural 41
merits, treasury of 49
monergism 79, 92, 110, 133; see also *cooperation with grace*
mortal sin – see *sin, mortal*
Moses 22, 26–28, 91–92, 122, 131
mystery 46, 93

Neo-Pelagianism – see *Pelagianism*
New Testament 62, 72
Newman, John Henry ix, 7, 60, 67, 83
nominalism 39
novelty 1, 6

Ockham, William of 39, 54, 95, 100
Oden, Thomas C. 4–5
Office of the Keys, 47, 103
Old Testament law – see *Law, Old Testament*
Old Testament saints 40
On the Spirit and the Letter 3, 141–45
ontology 16–17, 91, 97, 111
Origen 4–5
orthodoxy, pillars of 7

papal infallibility 60, 62, 64–65, 73–74
paradox 46
pastoral practice 53, 60, 130–31
Paul 22–28, 42, 46, 49, 51, 52n33, 62, 66, 70, 73, 81, 83, 90, 96, 102, 110, 117–28, 132–33, 135–40
Peirce, C. S. 67
Pelagianism 19, 40, 95, 99–100, 107, 115
penalty, eternal 46–49

General Index

temporal xii-xiii, 47–50, 81, 90, 103–4
Penance 6, 47, 87, 104
penitence 35
perseverance, 45, 51, 113
Peter 9, 44, 57, 63, 81–84
phenomenology 16
Pius IX, Pope 78
Plato 32
pope xiii, 81–82
praying to the saints, 76–78
precepts of Church 35
predestination – see *election*
Preus, Robert 3n5, 15n4, 31–32, 63–64
punishment – see *penalty*
purgatory xi-xiii, 20, 48–49, 75–76

Quenstedt, Johannes Andreas 15, 63, 66–67

rebirth – see *regeneration*
Reconciliation (sacrament) 6, 34, 42, 46–47, 51, 53, 87, 103–4
Reformation x-xii, 8, 48, 75–6, 87
regeneration 2, 13, 18–20, 24–25, 29, 31, 37, 39, 53–54, 56, 96, 99, 111, 114, 124, 127–28, 144
remission of sins – see *forgiveness*
remnant 8
reward 3, 13, 24–5, 29, 38–39, 41–43, 56–57, 105–6, 115, 129, 137, 140, 144
righteousness of Christ – see *Christ, righteousness of*
righteousness,
 alien/external vs. internal 2, 16–18, 20, 56–57, 105, 114, 118, 120, 132, 136, 141–45
 extrinsic vs. intrinsic 15–7, 32
 imputed 13–16, 18–20, 39, 56, 89–91, 101, 111, 114, 143
rigorism 47
ritual 23, 26–7, 34

sacraments 6, 12–3, 34, 47, 51, 53–54, 71, 85, 87, 100–101, 112
sacrifice of the Mass xiii, 80–1
saints – see *praying to the saints*
salvation
 assurance of 50–52, 100–101, 104, 110, 112–13
 by grace 22, 76
 final 11, 46, 113, 128
 loss of 41, 44–45, 103, 114
sanctification 10, 12, 20, 45–47, 50, 58, 76, 95–96, 101–2, 111, 127, 132–35; see also *justification*
Sanders, E. P. 22n15
satisfaction xiii, 36n24, 46–47, 55, 81, 96, 103–4
Scaer, David P. 138–39
Scotus, John Duns 100
Scripture, canon of 8, 63, 66–67, 71
Scriptures 7, 25–26, 59
 perspicuity of 63–64
 silence of 68, 77
self-righteousness 50, 53, 130–31
Semi-Pelagianism – see *Pelagianism*
sin 45–46, 89–90, 108–9, 121
 mortal 3, 35, 52n33, 98, 103–5, 112, 115, 131
 venial 42n27, 90, 102–3
sinlessness 15, 76, 78, 91, 121

General Index

Smalcald Articles 76
Small Catechism (Luther's) 52n33, 94
sola fide –see *justification by faith alone*
sola gratia 46; see also *grace*
sola scriptura xi, 59–74
solo Christo 36, 48, 98, 111
Spirit, fruit of the – see *fruit of the Spirit*
Spirit, gift of the 13, 20
suffering 49
synergism – see *monergism*

temporal penalty –see *penalty, temporal*
Tolkien, J. R. R. 79
Torah—see *Law, Old Testament*
Tradition 59–60, 62, 65–67
tradition, Rabbinic 62
Trent, Council of xii, 4, 12, 19, 35–38, 41–44, 54, 89–116, 118, 127
Trinity ix, 7, 67

union with Christ 16–20, 32, 34, 98, 106, 111, 116, 120, 123
unity of Church –see *Church, unity of*
universalism 33, 57, 94

Vatican II 40, 60, 81,
virtue 32–33, 55

Walther, C. F. W. 35
Word of God 59, 62, 64, 71
work of the law – see *law, work of*
works, good – see *good works*
wrath of God, 49, 76, 91
Wright, N T xiin1, 22

Zetterholm, Magnus xiin1

www.ingramcontent.com/pod-product-compliance
Lightning Source LLC
Chambersburg PA
CBHW030857170426
43193CB00009BA/644